The New
Brown Bag

The Talking Stick

The New
Brown Bag

The Talking Stick
40 Children's Sermons
with Activities

Randy Hammer

THE
PILGRIM
PRESS
Cleveland

As I work on stories and lessons for children week after week, I have but
one regret, that I did not take the opportunity to write and read more
stories to my own children when they were young. Often feeling that I
was too busy with schoolwork and church work, or that my children did
not care whether I read them stories or not (a false assumption on my
part), or that it was not that important, I lost some valuable opportunities to teach and touch and strengthen familial bonds with my children,
Nathanael and Kristin. So I dedicate this book especially to them, as well
as to their children, my grandchildren, with whom I hope to spend many
fine hours of reading stories together.

The Pilgrim Press, 700 Prospect Avenue, Cleveland, OH 44115-1100
thepilgrimpress.com

Some of the stories, the bulleted list in the introduction, and material in the
annotated resource list appeared in Randy Hammer, *Everyone a Butterfly: 40 Sermons
for Children*, Boston: Skinner House, 2004. Used by permission of the publisher.

Library of Congress Cataloging-in-Publication Data

Hammer, Randy, 1955–
      The talking stick : forty children's sermons with activities / Randy Hammer.
          p.   cm.   (The new brown bag)
      Includes bibliographical references.
      ISBN 978-0-8298-1761-4 (alk. paper)
      1. Children's sermons.   2. Church year sermons.   I. Title.

BV4315.H2785 2007
252'.53—dc22

                                                              2006037287

Contents

Preface

Everyone loves a story, children and adults alike. People can be daydreaming along through a sermon until the preacher begins to transition into a story, and then a visible change occurs across the congregation. People sit up straighter, raise their heads higher, and perk up their ears to listen. Indeed, one well-known preacher and much sought after seminar and workshop leader in America today has described the successful sermon as "a story wrapped around an image."[1]

Hence, those brief moments in the weekend worship service variously known as "Children's Parable," "Children's Time," or "Children's Sermon" hold much opportunity for speaking to, moving, educating, challenging, indeed transforming children of all ages. Though I prepare children's sermons with children in mind (as it should be done), it is not uncommon for adult congregants to tell me following the Sunday morning worship service, "I like (or learn from) the children's parable more than the sermon." I usually take it as a compliment, especially if that children's parable was one I worked long and hard on. In fact, usually the children's story comes with much more difficulty for me than does the "adult" sermon. Whereas by midweek I generally have the "adult" sermon for the upcoming Sunday's service pretty much in final form, I sometimes find myself on Saturday fretting over what I am going to say to the children in less than twenty-four hours. The five- to ten-minute period in the worship service when the children come up front for their special time requires as much thought, reverence, and care as the other fifty minutes or so do, perhaps more; because in that period of time, brief as it may seem, we are responsible for helping mold growing, inquisitive minds.

I am constantly reminded of how carefully my words must be chosen and how dangerous it sometimes is to speak off the cuff. Children tend to take what I say seriously! Once just after Christmas a child asked during the children's parable when we were going to place the Wise Men around the nativity. I replied casually to all the children, "I have it on good authority that the Wise Men will be coming next Sunday" (which was Epiphany Sunday). I meant that then we would bring the ceramic figures of the Magi and camels out of hiding and place them around the nativity set as we had done all the other characters at the close of the children's parable a few Sundays prior. One child didn't forget that. After the worship service the following Sunday, that disappointed child said to his parents, "I thought *real* Wise Men were coming to church today; but all I got to do was place an old camel at the nativity set." We best be careful what we say and how we say it. Such takes much thought, careful preparation, and a wise choice of words.

Many of the stories and lessons to be found in this small volume have been labored over and shared with children of all ages at First Congregational Church, United Church of Christ, of Albany, New York. I have sought to "wrap stories around an image." The outline of the work follows the church and calendar year, beginning in September. There are stories and lessons that may be used for Labor Day, starting back to school, World Communion Day, stewardship season, Reformation Sunday, Halloween, Advent, Christmas, New Year, Epiphany, Valentine's Day, Christian Unity, Lent, Palm Sunday, Easter, spring, Memorial Day, and Pentecost. You will find stories and lessons here that acquaint hearers with historic figures like Brother Lawrence, Martin Luther, Phyllis Wheatley, and Louis Braille. These stories and lessons seek to instill respect for all persons created in the divine image. They aim to encourage service, a positive approach to living, hospitality, unity and harmony, stewardship of the earth and our resources, authenticity and truthfulness, putting forth our best effort, personal sacrifice, peacemaking, evangelism, and spiritual self-improvement. And they occasionally draw a lesson from nature and science and are at all times in celebration of God's extravagant love.

Generally speaking, my preference in using scripture passages with children is the Good News Translation, because it is often considered particularly suitable for children. However, occasionally a different translation is preferred, most often the New Revised Standard

Version. For each scriptural basis of the stories included, the suggested translation is noted.

I would also like to take this opportunity to express appreciation to editor Mary Benard and the rest of the staff at Skinner House Books for granting permission to draw from *Everyone a Butterfly: 40 Sermons for Children*, my first collection of children's sermons, which they saw fit to publish in 2004.

May you and your children find within these pages resources that will result in many quality hours of story time together.

Introduction

How Do Children's Sermons Come About?

How does one go about writing a children's sermon? First, become so familiar with the following characteristics that make for a quality children's sermon that they become second nature. I discussed these in some detail in my first published collection of children's sermons: *Everyone a Butterfly: 40 Sermons for Children*, which constituted my Doctor of Ministry project in ministry. A quality children's sermon:

- Is not condescending
- Is concerned with universal truth and universal human need
- Sparks children's imagination
- Nourishes self-understanding
- Enables children to relate positively to the world around them
- Is simple, centered around a single truth
- Speaks to all ages in the congregation
- Does not get a laugh at the children's expense
- Appeals to as many of the senses as possible
- Is an appropriate length, generally seven to eight minutes
- Should be told and not read, if possible
- Should support the readings or theme of the day
- Should employ inclusive language[2]

Next, think about the children—their ages, interests, maturity—to prepare a suitable message that will pique their interest. Then isolate the topic or theme of the day. This may come from the Revised Common Lectionary readings for the day, be based on the church year, or be left to the discretion of the minister or worship leader.

Suppose the topic of the upcoming Sunday's service is peace (see chapter 19 of this book). Begin by brainstorming—calling on your experience, reading, and congregational resources—to come up with some possibilities. As I think about a message suitable for a group of children, mostly boys between the ages of six and twelve in our current congregation, the image of a police officer—a peace officer—comes to mind. A primary duty of the police officer is to help keep the peace. I recall that one of our members is a retired police officer. Here is a resource I can tap. I will probably ask to borrow that member's police officer's badge, which will be an object of interest to children of this age.

Then start drafting a message. Try speaking the words aloud, and begin by asking questions that will arouse curiosity. "Do you know what this is (hold up the badge)? Have any of you ever met a police officer? Do any of you know a police officer? What does a police officer do?" In this case, I decide to fabricate a story about a rowdy group of people who hold a noisy party way into the night with blasting music, shouting, breaking of bottles, use of foul language, and fighting. What would their neighbors do in such a situation? They would likely call the police—peace officers—who would come to help restore the peace. It might be emphasized that police officers as keepers of the peace perform a wonderful service for our communities.

From there I would share how, as people of faith, we are called to be peacemakers, to bring peace to our troubled world. I might note that working for peace is one of the primary objectives of the denomination to which we belong. I might ask the children to brainstorm about how all of us can work for peace in our homes and communities. After they have had time to respond, I might affirm that some steps that lead to peace in our daily lives include loving others as we want to be loved, forgiving others, doing to others as we want them to do unto us, seeking to be gentle and kind, and so forth.

To reinforce the message and give the children something to take with them to ponder throughout the week, plan a hands-on follow-up activity that focuses on symbols of peace, such as the dove or peace lily. For example, you might lead the children in planting or positioning a peace lily in a prominent place as an ongoing reminder that each of us is called to be a peacemaker.

As you may see, preparing children's sermons and stories is not an easy task—if they are done correctly. Perhaps this is why so many children's sermons that one can access online or find in ministers' resource books and magazines are shallow and unsuitable for general use. I have rarely found a children's sermon online (the few times I have looked) or in clergy journals and magazines that I felt comfortable using with no adaptation. More often than not I have run across an *idea* that I could glean and use as a seed to compose my own children's sermon that better said what I wanted to say.

It is my hope (based in part on positive responses from my first published collection) that the reader can use the children's sermons contained in this collection pretty much as they are in the book. But feel free to adapt. Perhaps even more important is the hope that these sermons and stories will stimulate imaginations so that readers may add their own contributions to this important genre of literature.

1
The Talking Stick
We Should Show Respect to Others and Listen When They Are Talking

SCRIPTURES: Proverbs 18:13 GNT; James 1:19 GNT

OBJECT FOR SHARING: Any kind of decorated stick that might be designated as the "talking stick of the day."

PRESENTATION: If possible, arrange the children in a circle so everyone can see everyone else. Share pictures of talking sticks from around the world from online websites. (Yahooing "talking sticks" yields a wealth of articles and pictures.) If time permits, at the close of the story pass the stick around the circle and invite each child to speak one sentence from the heart while holding the stick.

Have you ever seen one of these before? Do you know what this is? This is my "*talking* stick." Not a talking *stick*, but a *talking* stick. The stick does not talk, but it is to be held by someone who is talking. Let me explain.

Some cultures such as Native Americans and Hawaiians have the custom of passing a talking stick around the circle as different people speak to a group. The talking stick is usually about a foot long and decorated with symbols, or small pictures, important to those people. The leader of the meeting, perhaps the chief, might be the first to hold the stick and begin talking while everyone else listens.

Then the chief passes the stick to the next person on the right or left and everyone respectfully listens to that person and so on, until everyone who has anything to say has a chance to speak. No one can talk unless he or she is holding the stick. The idea is that the talking stick enables people to speak the truth from their heart and encourages everyone else to listen respectfully and compassionately. Each of us has a piece of truth to share with the group, but none of us has the whole truth. So I speak my truth, while you listen, and then you speak your truth while I listen. Sounds like a pretty good idea, huh, especially for those times like around the family dinner table when everyone is trying to talk at the same time and nobody is listening?

But we should not really have to have a talking stick for others to listen to us, should we? As followers of Jesus, we should try to always be respectful of others and listen carefully to what they are saying, and then hope that they do the same for us when it is our turn to speak. In several places the scriptures give wise advice about the importance of listening more than speaking.

But the talking stick has three important rules that we should always remember:

- We should speak honestly and truthfully from the heart.
- We should be brief, so everyone has a chance to speak.
- We should be quiet and listen carefully so we understand what others are saying.

FOLLOW-UP: Secure enough sticks (large wooden dowels if suitable natural sticks are not available) and paints so each child can create his or her own talking stick.

2

The Potato Peeler
We Can Find Joy
in Humble Service

SCRIPTURE: 2 Corinthians 5:14–15 GNT

OBJECTS FOR SHARING: A bowl, paring knife, and potato, which can be peeled in front of the children while the story is told.

PRESENTATION: This story works well near Labor Day or another day when service to others is being celebrated.

How many of you like to peel potatoes? (*Peel a potato over a bowl as you speak.*) Well, how many of you like to wash dishes? Today I have a story about someone who actually enjoyed doing both.

A long, long time ago, in the country of France, there lived a dedicated monk named Brother Lawrence. Can anyone tell us what a monk is? That's correct—a monk is someone who lives in a monastery with other monks and spends a lot of time praying, reading the scriptures, and serving other people. It is sort of like a lifelong church camp for grownups. But monks have to eat too, so many monks raise vegetable gardens, or tend honeybees, or take care of grapevines or fruit trees. And, of course, some of the monks have to work in the kitchen.

That's where Brother Lawrence comes in. Brother Lawrence was assigned to kitchen duty. This meant peeling potatoes and washing pots and pans and dishes. At first, Brother Lawrence didn't like kitchen work. But then Brother Lawrence decided to try to do everything that he did for the love of God. While he worked in the kitchen, he thought about his love for God and did his work as though he were actually doing it for God and not just for the other monks in the monastery. You know what? When Brother Lawrence learned to do his work out of his love for God and while he talked to God in prayer, he began to enjoy it.

Isn't there a lesson in Brother Lawrence's story for all of us? What are some of the jobs that all of us have to do around the house? (*Give time for answers.*) When we have to do our work around the house—whether it is helping in the kitchen, cleaning up our room, taking care of the family pet, or taking out the trash—if we can do it out of our love for God and our love for others, it is much easier to do.

FOLLOW-UP: 1) Assist the children in making potato ink stamps. 2) Lead the children in listing as many different kinds of service as possible that bless our lives. 3) Discuss how potatoes grow and their importance as a food source for much of the world.

3
What Are You Looking For?[3]
When It Comes to Others, We Often Find What We Are Looking For

SCRIPTURE: Luke 6:37–38 GNT

OBJECT FOR SHARING: A crossing guard sign to make the connection.

PRESENTATION: This story works well at the beginning of a new school year when many children are changing schools.

Once upon a time, a crossing guard helped children across the street to a certain school. While waiting for the traffic light to change, the crossing guard would often talk with the children and ask them questions. Sometimes the children asked questions of her.

One day, on the first day of a new school year, a new student came along and said to the crossing guard, "I'm new here. Can you tell me what kind of children go to school here?"

The crossing guard smiled, and then she said, "First, I have a question for you: Where did you come from?"

A little surprised, the child told her, "I come from Martha Washington School in Smithtown."

"Oh, Martha Washington School in Smithtown," the crossing guard replied. "Well, what kind of children went to *that* school?"

"Oh, you wouldn't believe how awful the children were at Martha Washington School," the child replied. "They were selfish, rude, unfriendly, and mean."

"My goodness!" replied the crossing guard. "Well, I am afraid I have bad news for you. I fear you will find the children in this school to be much the same as they were at Martha Washington School. I'm afraid you are going to have a difficult time here." The child went on to school disappointed and sulking.

A few minutes later, another new student came along. This student also said to the crossing guard, "I'm new here. Can you tell me what kind of children go here?"

The crossing guard smiled, and then she said, "First, I have a question for you: Where did you come from?"

A little surprised, the child told her, "I come from Martha Washington School in Smithtown."

"Oh, Martha Washington School in Smithtown," the crossing guard replied. "Well, what kind of children went to *that* school?"

"Oh, the children at Martha Washington School in Smithtown were wonderful. Everyone was so generous, polite, friendly, and helpful."

"Well," said the crossing guard, "then I have good news for you. I think you will find that the children at this school are just as generous, polite, friendly, and helpful as they were at Martha Washington School in Smithtown." And with that, this new student skipped toward the new school with a smile.

Jesus teaches us that the kind of attitude we have with others is the kind of attitude we will find. In other words, in life we often receive what we give. So if we expect other people to be generous, polite, friendly, and helpful with us, then we need to be generous, polite, friendly, and helpful with them.

FOLLOW-UP: Discuss how we often find in life what we are looking for. If we look for bad in others, we are sure to find it. If we look for good in others, we will find it as well. Discuss how we should look for the good in everyone, regardless of outward differences such as physical appearance, race, or ethnicity.

4
Eric Faces the Giant
Love Is the Most Powerful Force and Best Course of Action

SCRIPTURES: Proverbs 25:21 GNT; Matthew 5:42–44 GNT

OBJECT FOR SHARING: A popular style of lunchbox.

PRESENTATION: This story works well at the beginning of the new school year, when some children may be apprehensive about starting or starting back to school.

Eric was standing at the street corner waiting to get on the school bus. Eric hated getting on the school bus. Practically every morning he developed an upset stomach, what his teacher sometimes referred to as "Yellow Bus Fever." He would much rather stay home.

One of the things that made it so bad was that every morning when he got on the school bus he had to face that giant bully—Frankie Valentine. Frankie Valentine was four grades ahead of Eric and about twice his size. By the time Eric got on the bus, all the front seats were taken, which meant he had to go toward the back of the bus, where Frankie Valentine sat. As soon as Eric neared Frankie's seat, he would stick his giant leg out, barricading the aisle.

"What you got in your lunchbox for me today?" Frankie snarled practically every morning. If Eric didn't open his lunchbox and let Frankie go through it and pick out what he wanted, Frankie would sock him in the stomach with his fist. The bus driver was too busy keeping his eyes on the street to notice.

Again this day Frankie stuck out his giant leg, blocked the aisle, and held out his hand for Eric's lunchbox. And again Eric handed it over. Frankie found the Little Debbie cake his mom had packed for his lunch, quickly stripped it of its wrapper, and wolfed it down in a second. With a sly grin he closed the lunchbox, shoved it in Eric's stomach, and let him pass on by.

That afternoon when he came home from school, Eric was visibly upset. He began to cry. When questioned, Eric told his mom how every day Frankie took part of his lunch or socked him in the stomach if he refused to give it up. Eric's mom put her arm around him, as tears formed in her own eyes.

After thinking about the situation a few minutes, Eric's mom said, "Eric, I know Frankie's parents. They have both been out of work for a while. They must be having it rough at home. Maybe they don't have enough to eat. Sometimes bullies really are not bad people deep down inside. Sometimes difficult circumstances make people do hurtful things. Let me think about this overnight and then we'll talk about it in the morning."

Eric went to bed that night feeling somewhat better. But in the morning when he awoke, that same old upset tummy feeling was back. He didn't want to catch the school bus. But as soon as he sat down at the breakfast table, he spied something strange. Instead of one lunchbox sitting on the table for him to take to school, there were two. "Mom, why are there *two* lunchboxes sitting there?"

"Well, Eric, I thought and prayed about your problem with Frankie. And I remembered something that Jesus said: 'When someone asks you for something, give it to him; when someone wants to borrow something, lend it to him. Love your enemies and pray for those who persecute you.' Instead of being angry at Frankie, let's try loving him and see what happens."

Eric was not so sure about this plan, but he agreed to try it. What did he have to lose? So when he climbed up on the bus that morning, Frankie was waiting on him, as always. But this time Eric didn't dread walking back Frankie's way. In fact, he walked back through the bus a little faster than usual. Before Frankie could even put his giant leg out in the aisle and reach out for Eric's lunchbox, Eric stuck the second lunchbox out toward Frankie and said, "Here, Frankie; my mom and I want you to have this."

A strange look came over Frankie's face. He didn't know what to say. Frankie's tone softened. "Well, thanks, Eric." That's all the words Frankie could get out. He took the lunchbox and carefully opened it to find two sandwiches, a big, red apple, a bag of chips, and a Little Debbie cake. Frankie closed the lid of the lunchbox and said, "This is really nice. I'm going to save it all for lunch." And then he sat back in his seat to think about stuff. Eric walked on by and took his seat and thought about stuff, too.

That afternoon, when it was time for Eric to get off the bus, Frankie put his giant leg out in the aisle and stopped him. Then with a big smile he gave Eric the empty lunchbox, moved his leg out of the way and said, "Tell your mom I said thanks for the lunch. That was really nice of her. And tomorrow morning, I'm saving you a seat right here beside me. How about we be friends from now on?"

FOLLOW-UP: Invite the children to share stories of times when they felt bullied, how they responded, and how they might have responded differently.

5
The Hospitable Squirrel
It Is Important to Welcome Newcomers

SCRIPTURE: Matthew 25:34–40 GNT

OBJECTS FOR SHARING: A variety of nuts that might be gathered by squirrels.

PRESENTATION: This story works best in October or November, when squirrels are busy preparing for winter.

Have you been noticing the squirrels lately? I have. I have been noticing busy squirrels everywhere I go. What do you suppose they are up to? Well, today I have a story about a busy squirrel.

Once there was a busy squirrel. Since his tail was so full and bushy, that's what the other squirrels called him—Bushy. Now Bushy was a hardworking squirrel. When it was time to build a nest, Bushy built the biggest, nicest, prettiest, and warmest nest in the forest. When it came time to prepare for winter, Bushy worked night and day gathering nuts and storing them in his hollow tree, sometimes while all the other squirrels were playing and chasing each other through the branches.

When the first snow of the season started to fall, Bushy was content in his nice, big, warm nest with his hollow tree full of nuts close by. Pretty soon Bushy's squirrel friends started to stop by to hang out at his nest. "My, what a nice stash of nuts you have," some of them exclaimed. Bushy's nest was so inviting, and his store of nuts was so big, that pretty soon squirrels and more squirrels were making themselves at home with him. There were so many squirrels and there was always so much cheerful squirrel chatter that it seemed like Bushy and his friends were having a never-ending party.

Well, how do you suppose Bushy felt about all the other squirrels coming to his nest and sharing in his store of nuts? Bushy was not upset or jealous at all. Because, you see, Bushy liked the company and the fellowship. As far as he was concerned, the more squirrels that came to his nest, the merrier.

Do you suppose that Bushy has something to teach us about Sunday school and church? We are interested in seeing our Sunday school grow, aren't we? We want new people to come to the "nest" that we have built. It is important that we, like Bushy, welcome all new children who come here. It is important that we are eager to share goodies at coffee hour. And it is important that we let all new children know we're glad they're here.

One of the things that Jesus teaches us is that we should always be careful about welcoming the new person who comes into our midst. When we welcome someone new, it is like welcoming Jesus himself.

FOLLOW-UP: If possible, take the children on a field trip to see a squirrel's nest.

6
Playing in Harmony
It Is Much More Beautiful When We All Work Together

SCRIPTURES: Psalm 133:1 GNT; Ephesians 5:19 NRSV

OBJECT FOR SHARING: An Appalachian dulcimer or other such interesting instrument that easily can be taken out of tune and back in tune again.

PRESENTATION: This story works well on World Communion Sunday or Christian Unity Sunday. This story will be even more effective if a musician "unexpectedly" joins the children to participate.

Good morning! Oh, Fred, what do you have there?

"This is called a dulcimer."

A dulcimer, you say. That's an odd looking sort of thing. Tell us a little about it.

"Well, the dulcimer is an instrument that originated a couple of hundred years ago in the Appalachian Mountains. You see, it is tuned so that one need only to strike the strings to play a beautiful melody *(musician plays a few chords)*. But watch what happens if I turn the tuning screws a bit" *(musician strums the now out-of-tune strings)*.

Wait a minute, Fred. That didn't sound so good. What happened?

"Well, when all the strings work together, the result is beautiful music. But when some of the strings decide to go their own way, well, you heard what happens. It is sort of like when all of us sing on the same note. It makes for beautiful singing. But what if all of us decided to sing whatever note we wanted to? Wouldn't that sound terrible?"

I see what you mean. You know, we can take this a step further and see how it applies to the unity or harmony of the church. When all of us work together, beautiful things can be accomplished. But should all of us insist on having our own way, well, that could be disastrous.

On a day like World Communion Day, it reminds us that we also need to work together in harmony with all Christians and all churches, because we can do many good things together in the world that we could never do apart. It truly is beautiful when brothers and sisters live and work together in harmony!

Thanks, Fred, for the lesson about the dulcimer. How about playing a few chords as the children return to the seats.

FOLLOW-UP: Invite the musician to continue the instrument lesson and tell different ways the instrument has been used—folk music, sacred music, and so on. Lead the children in exploring other examples of things that teach the importance of working together.

7
Giving to God First
The Importance of Stewardship and Giving

SCRIPTURE: 1 Corinthians 16:2 GNT

OBJECT FOR SHARING: A wallet or purse containing enough one-dollar bills so every child can be given one.

PRESENTATION: This lesson is intended for the time when the church is emphasizing its annual stewardship campaign, for most churches in the fall. In distributing the bills, it is to appear that the presenter runs out before the last one and gives that child (or adult, if you need more participants) a small coin. You may or may not want to hand pick the last person and have him or her sit on the end of the row, explaining the lesson beforehand.

Good morning. You are going to be glad that you came to church and to the children's parable today. Because I am feeling generous. I am going to give each of you a one-dollar bill *(start at the opposite end of the row or circle from the one where you want to end up, giving each child a one-dollar bill, except for the last one)*. Oh no! I seemed to have run out of dollar bills. I am so sorry, Monica. But I can give you this small coin. You will be happy with that, won't you? *(Depending on your prior coaching, the person who received the coin may act disappointed, sad, or upset.)*

Monica, you seem to be unhappy. Would you like to tell us how you feel? *(Give a moment for the person to share.)*

Boys and girls, pretend with me this morning that Monica is God, because in a lot of ways God is the One who comes last. We buy food, we go to the movies, we go out to eat, we pay for our car or bicycle, and then if we have anything left, then we give that small portion to God. How do you suppose that makes God feel?

But I have a better idea. But you are going to have to trust me. I need everyone to give the one-dollar bills back to me *(collect the bills, and if some object, try to assure them that they will get it back. Put all the bills back into the wallet or purse, and then pull all of the bills out, including the one that was previously held back, and start distributing them with the person representing God).*

Okay, here is what I am going to do. This time I am going to start with Monica, who is playing the part of God. Before we give to anyone else, we are going to give to God first. *(Begin giving out the bills again. The child on the opposite end may look sad or disturbed; if so, flash him or her an assuring smile).* Well, would you look at that! This time *everyone* received a dollar bill. If we make a point to always give to God first from what we have to give, it just may be that we don't miss what we give to God and still have enough to do all the other things we want to do.

FOLLOW-UP: Lead the children in looking up in a Bible concordance verses having to do with tithing and proportionate giving. Lead a discussion about different percentages of giving based on the money the children make or allowances they receive.

8
The Sharecropper
We Are to Care
for the Earth

SCRIPTURES: Psalm 24:1 GNT; 1 Corinthians 4:2 NRSV

OBJECT FOR SHARING: Ears of field corn, which can usually be found in autumn at farmers' markets.

PRESENTATION: This story works well in the autumn around harvest time, a time when many churches are emphasizing stewardship.

Does anyone know what a sharecropper is? Well, there aren't as many sharecroppers today as there once were. A landowner provides the farmland, and maybe the seed to plant a crop, and the sharecropper does all the work and then shares in the profit at harvest time. Today I have a story about a landowner and some sharecroppers.

Once upon a time, a wealthy landowner had a hundred acres that he wanted planted in corn. So one day in the spring, he went to the village and asked for someone who would like to plant his crop. Finding a willing worker, the landowner took him to his home, showed him the land, and gave him the corn seed. He asked only that the sharecropper respect him and his land and do his best to produce a good crop. Well, the next day the sharecropper went to another village and sold half of the corn seed and kept the money for himself. He then planted the other half. When the corn grew and was ready for harvest, the landowner couldn't understand. "Where is the rest of my crop?" the landowner cried. "There should have been twice this much corn."

"I don't know," the sharecropper lied. "I planted the corn seed, and this is all that grew." The landowner was very unhappy, feeling that something must not be right.

The next spring the landowner did the same thing. He went to the village and found another sharecropper to plant his corn. Again he asked only that the sharecropper respect him and his land and do his best to produce a good crop. This sharecropper planted all the corn seed, plowed the corn and raised a good crop. But just before harvest time, he took money from a busload of high school students who wanted to make a corn maze in the field. So the young persons went in the field and trampled down half of the corn. When the share-cropper and landowner took what was left to the market, there was only half as much as there should have been. Again the landowner was very unhappy and thought something must not be right.

The third year the landowner again went to the village and found a sharecropper to plant his crop. All he asked was that the share-cropper would respect him and his land and do the best he could to produce a good crop. This year the sharecropper planted all the seed, plowed the field to keep out the weeds, kept wild animals out of the field, and guarded the corn day and night. When they took the crop to market, it was more than twice it had been the two years before. The landowner was very happy and knew that at last he had found someone he could trust. For many years the two worked together and both were very happy.

Now, this story is a parable. A long, long time ago, God created the world and all that is in it and gave it to men and women, boys and girls to use and enjoy. God said, "Here is the land. Grow your food, gather the fruit, enjoy the streams and the oceans. I only ask that you respect me and respect my land and return to me a fair offering from what you earn." But you know what? Men and women, boys and girls have not always respected the land that belongs to God. The earth has been made dirty; the streams, lakes, and oceans have been pol-luted; and we often forget to return to God a fair offering from what we earn. God doesn't ask for one-half like the landowner in the story. In fact, God would be happy with just 10 percent.

So you see, God is the landowner and we are sort of like share-croppers. We don't own the land; we just borrow it from God.

FOLLOW-UP: 1) Discuss the miracle of growth, how the corn seed is planted, sprouts, grows, and reproduces manyfold. 2) Discuss various ways we can better care for the earth.

9
Things That Make Us Think
Things That Happen Often Make Us Think about Our Relationship with God

SCRIPTURES: Romans 8:28 GNT; Philippians 2:13 GNT

OBJECT FOR SHARING: A minister's red stole.

PRESENTATION: This story works best on Reformation Sunday, the last Sunday of October. Play "A Mighty Fortress Is Our God" as a hymn prior to the children's story.

Good morning! How many of you have ever been struck by lightning? Well, how many of you have ever been knocked to the ground? Most of us have been knocked to the ground or fallen to the ground, haven't we? Well, today I have a story about someone who got knocked to the ground and then went on to change the world.

Once upon a time, a long, long time ago, a young university student, twenty-one years old, was walking down a dirt road. The young man's name was Martin.

As Martin walked along, probably in deep thought about his studies, clouds started to gather in the sky. A few drops of rain began to fall. All of sudden, a streak of lightning jumped down from the sky and struck a nearby tree. The lightning was so close, Martin was knocked to the ground. He was terrified, as you might imagine. And without even really thinking about it, Martin looked up at the sky and yelled, "I will become a monk!" (*Can anyone tell us what a monk is?*) A monk is someone who goes to live in a special place where everyone spends a lot of time studying the Bible and praying.

Well, Martin did become a monk. And there was no monk better than Monk Martin. He studied the Bible. He prayed all the time. He fasted—or went without food—in order to show God how hard he was trying to be a good man. But in spite of all his praying, and studying, and fasting, Monk Martin just couldn't seem to be satisfied. He never did feel like he was being good enough for God.

Then one day while Monk Martin was studying the Bible, he discovered a little word called "faith." It was like Martin had been made a new man. Because he now realized that even though we can never be perfect, God still loves us and it is our faith, our *faithfulness*, and not our perfect lives, that pleases God.

Can anyone guess what Martin's last name was? It was Luther. His name was Martin Luther, the man who helped start what is called the Protestant Reformation. Martin Luther wrote the hymn we sang earlier, "A Mighty Fortress Is Our God." On this Sunday many ministers wear red stoles in honor of Martin Luther and others like him. Now, there are two things about Martin's story that apply to you and me. First, sometimes things happen in our lives that lead us to think about our relationship with God and cause us to ask if there is something that God wants us to do. Sometimes even bad things that happen to us can be turned into something good.

And second, Martin's life was changed while he was studying the Bible. That's what studying the Bible does for us—it helps us to understand and changes us into better men and women, better boys and girls.

We don't want to be knocked down by lightning like Martin, do we? But we can learn from Martin about studying the Bible and about having faith in God.

FOLLOW-UP: Explain further the reason for wearing a red stole on Reformation Sunday, how the color red stands for the blood of the martyrs, other reformers who gave their lives to improve the church.

10
Taking Off Our Mask
It Is Important to Be
Who We Claim to Be

Scripture: Matthew 23:27–28 GNT

Object for Sharing: If available, a papier-mâché art mask, with the two sides painted differently (as indicated in the story) or an appropriate Halloween mask.

Presentation: This story work bests the Sunday just prior to Halloween.

Good morning! There is something that a lot of people wear at this time of year. That's right—a mask. What are we really doing when we wear a mask? We are pretending to be someone or something we are not. Can you think of some of the things we pretend to be when we put on a mask? (*Give a moment for answers.*)

I have brought a mask with me this morning. (*Hold up your mask.*) What do you notice about this mask? The two sides of the face are different, aren't they? This mask was created to show the difference between the way we sometimes are on the inside, which may be different from the way we appear on the outside. Or to put it another way, sometimes people pretend to be something or someone they are not. It's sort of like they are wearing a mask.

For instance, have you ever known someone whom you thought was your friend, but then later you learned that that person did something behind your back—maybe made fun of you to other people—something that showed that they really were not your friend? On the outside they were wearing the face or mask of a friend. But on the inside they were something different.

One can also wear the mask of being a lover of God or follower of Jesus on the outside, but on the inside not really love God or be a follower of Jesus at all. They are just pretending. Jesus warned about the habit of pretending to be something on the outside that we are not really on the inside.

Wearing Halloween masks is fun for all of us. And that is well and good. What is really important is that we not wear a false face in real life, pretending to be someone we are not. Rather, it is important that we always be who we claim to be and who we really are on the inside.

FOLLOW-UP: Secure papier-mâché masks and acrylic paints from an art supply store and encourage the children to paint the mask of the person they are inside.

11
Giving Our Best
Whatever We Are Called to Be or Do in Life Deserves Our Best Effort

SCRIPTURES: 1 Timothy 4:14 GNT; 2 Timothy 1:5–7 GNT

OBJECTS FOR SHARING: A golf club, or putter, and golf ball (you might want to use a plastic one).

PRESENTATION: This story works well during the church's stewardship season, when the sharing of gifts is emphasized.

(As the children are coming forward, begin by silently taking the stance as though you are going to swing at a golf ball.) Oh, good morning! How many of you play golf (look for show of hands)? Well, how many of you have played miniature golf or putt putt? Miniature golf is about my speed.

But if I were to ask you to name one of the most famous golfers in America today, who would you say? Someone said Tiger Woods. That is a good answer. What do you think makes Tiger Woods so special? Well, not only was Tiger the first African American to ever win the Masters Golf Tournament, he was also the youngest man to do so, at the age of twenty-one. But on top of that, he won the Masters Golf Tournament with the best score in history!

Now, what was it that helped Tiger Woods be such a winner at golf? I think dedication had a lot to do with it. For, you see, Tiger began his journey of becoming a professional golfer at the age of *(anyone want to guess?)*—three. And all his life Tiger was dedicated to the game of golf and being the very best golfer that he could be.

Now, you and I may not be destined to be professional golfers. At least, I know I am not. But you and I are gifted to do other things. I learned that one of my gifts is preaching *(or whatever gift the leader might have)*. What do you think that one of your gifts might be?

In the Bible we read about a young man named Timothy. At a young age, Timothy discovered that he had a gift for ministry and leadership. A wise leader in the church wrote to Timothy and told him to always remember the gift that he had been given and not be shy about using his gift just because he was young.

One of the great joys that we have here at church as you grow up and continue your education is helping you discover the gifts that you have been given so that you can find your place of service in the world.

But the primary point that I want to make today is no matter what gift we may have, each of us is called to do our very best in developing that gift as we use that gift in the service of God.

FOLLOW-UP: Lead the children in naming other young persons or young adults who are famous for their gifts. Then explore ways that persons in prominent positions can use their gifts and positions to accomplish good (being vocal and advocating for justice, environmental concerns, and the like; giving a portion of their earnings to charity; being mentors to underprivileged children; and so on).

12
The Big Job of Little Leaves
Each of Us Has a Contribution to Make to the Whole

SCRIPTURE: Proverbs 30:24–28 GNT

OBJECTS FOR SHARING: A variety of fresh, fall leaves in as many colors and shapes as possible.

PRESENTATION: This story works best in the fall but may be used any time when there is an adequate supply of leaves.

Do you like leaves? I love leaves. In fact, probably everyone likes leaves—except when we have to rake and bag them.

One of the interesting things about leaves is that they are all different. Just like snowflakes, no two leaves are exactly alike. Some are red and some are yellow, some are green and some are orange. But they are also different in size and shape.

What are leaves good for? Have you ever thought about it? Well, besides giving us shade in the summer time and being pretty in the fall, leaves have a very important job to do. And all leaves have the same purpose—to make food for the tree by using water, sunlight, and carbon dioxide. Without the food that the leaves produce, the tree could not grow, or even live. The giant oak or maple tree is dependent upon tiny leaves like this one to provide food.

You know, a church is sort of like a tree, and its members are sort of like leaves. Every one of us has something to give to the church to help keep it healthy and make it grow. Though we may feel that our efforts are small, whatever time or talent or offering we can give to the church is important. There are a lot of insects, animals, and plants in the world that are very small but still very important to the proper working of God's creation. And when the time, talents, and offerings of all of us are put together, no matter how small we may think them to be, they make a great difference in the life of our church. The church, in turn—like a tree—can provide food, shelter, and joy to all of us.

The Bible talks about a number of things that are small but are nevertheless important. Leaves could be added to the list of small, but very important things. So when you look up at the leaves, remember how that each and every leaf has an important part to play in the life of that tree. But even greater is the important part that *you* have to play in the life of our church.

FOLLOW-UP: 1) Have the children learn more about the important work of leaves, not only in providing food for the tree, but also producing oxygen for us to breathe. 2) Lead them in laminating leaves to make bookmarks, placemats, Thanksgiving cards, and the like.

13
Many Ways to Honor God
Regardless of Our Job or Talent, We Often Can Find a Way to Honor God

SCRIPTURE: Matthew 20:26b–28 GNT

OBJECTS FOR SHARING: A shoe last (perhaps can be borrowed from a local shoe repair shop), small hammer, and shoe.

PRESENTATION: Have all objects hidden in a secret bag or box. Bring them out in the order suggested.

Good morning! I am guessing that you may not have one of these *(bring shoe last base from bag)* in your living room or on your kitchen table. Can anyone guess what this might be? Okay, what if we add this *(bring shoe mold from bag)*—now can you guess what this might be? That's right—this is called a shoe last, and it is used by someone who repairs shoes.

Many years ago, during the Great Depression in the late 1920s and early 1930s, and then again during the Second World War, many people didn't have money to buy new shoes. And because so many materials like leather went to the war effort, shoes were hard to find anyway. So families often had to repair their own shoes. When the heel came off or a hole wore in the sole, the father or mother put the shoe on the shoe last and nailed on a new heel or patched the sole. *(Place shoe on the last and remove the hammer and pound on the shoe heel a bit.)*

But you know what? There are some people who spend their entire lives repairing shoes. Can anyone tell us the name for someone who repairs shoes? It is a cobbler. Some people feel that it is their talent, their calling in life, to repair shoes. In fact, engraved on a gravestone in a churchyard in England is this verse: "Here lies the body of John Smith, who for forty years cobbled shoes in this village to the glory of God."

The great lesson that we learn in this is that almost any job or task that we might have in life—as long as we truly feel that this is our gift and calling—can be used to serve other people and bring honor to God. When we use our gift to serve other people, then we are doing as Jesus has done. And that is a good thing. The important thing is that we perform our task with joy and enthusiasm and in humility do it for others and offer it as a service to God.

FOLLOW-UP: Secure an old shoe and some small shoe nails and allow each child to help "repair" the sole of a shoe to instill an appreciation for those who engage in this profession.

14
A Cup of Cold Water
By Sharing the Gift of Drinking Water, We Can Minister to Christ

SCRIPTURES: Matthew 10:40, 42; 25:35 GNT

OBJECTS FOR SHARING: A clear pitcher of cool water and small cups so each child can be given a drink at the close of the story.

PRESENTATION: This story works well when stewardship or missions is the theme of the day.

Do you ever get thirsty? Of course you do. We all get really thirsty sometimes. Can you name some of the times when you have gotten really thirsty? Has anyone ever gotten so thirsty that you thought you might pass out? That can be scary, can't it? It is important when we are out in the sun in the hot summertime to be sure that we drink enough water to keep ourselves hydrated. Losing too much water from our bodies too fast without putting it back in can be dangerous.

In Jesus' day people often traveled on foot in the hot sun from one village or town to another. As you can imagine, they got quite thirsty on the way. So when they arrived at their destination, they were ready for a cold drink of water. And just as people today work in the fields in the hot sun and get very thirsty—such as the people who plant and harvest the food we eat—they also did in Jesus' day. It has always been that way, and probably always will be.

So Jesus knew the importance of giving a cold drink of water to those who are thirsty. And Jesus said, "Whoever gives even a drink of cold water to one of the least of these my followers because he is my follower, will certainly receive a reward" (Matt. 10:42 GNT). In fact, when we give someone who is thirsty a cold drink of water, it is almost like we are giving it to Jesus himself (Matt. 25:35).

So the next time someone you know says, "I'm really thirsty," that is great opportunity for you to be of service and offer them the gift of a cold glass of water. When we give such an important gift, we can offer it as a gift to Jesus himself.

FOLLOW-UP: Help the children become familiar with various mission opportunities and organizations such as Church World Service, which help peoples in developing countries achieve clean drinking water. Perhaps the children will want to start a mission fund drive to be given toward helping a village achieve the goal of clean drinking water.

15
Preparing the Manger
Advent Is a Time to Make Preparations in Our Hearts and Lives

SCRIPTURE: 1 Peter 3:15 GNT

OBJECT FOR SHARING: A nativity set.

PRESENTATION: Ideally, this story is for the first Sunday of Advent. Find a place in the worship space or home where the nativity set can be displayed throughout Advent. Only display the shed and a couple of animals—perhaps a sheep and cow—and a shepherd out of view until the appropriate time; otherwise, the children will be distracted. Add a couple of characters each week, holding the baby Jesus until Christmas Eve or Christmas Day and the Magi until Epiphany (twelve days after Christmas, if you want to be liturgically correct; otherwise put them out on Christmas Eve or Christmas Day as well).

Today is the first Sunday of Advent, a period of four weeks before Christmas, when we celebrate the birth of Jesus. One of the things that some churches, and some families, do during this season is prepare the manger for the baby Jesus, who comes on Christmas Eve or Christmas Day. So each of the four Sundays during Advent we will place a couple of animals or characters in or around the manger to get it ready for baby Jesus.

But preparing the manger is really a way to remind us about the need for something much bigger and greater—preparing our hearts and lives to celebrate the birth of Jesus. As one of the Christmas hymns that we sing says, "Let every heart prepare him room."

Why do you think we need to prepare our hearts and lives for Christmas? (*Give time for reflection and such answers as busy schedules, etc.*) Good answers.

In what ways can we prepare our hearts and lives to celebrate the birth of Jesus? (*Give time for reflection and answers such as meditation, prayer, attending Christmas services, giving to the less fortunate, etc.*) Great!

Now we will start with our youngest one and let you place an animal where you think it should be placed around the manger. (*Assist the child or two or three of the children in placing a cow, sheep, shepherd, etc. in front of the manger.*)

But let us remember in the days between each Sunday of Advent to also prepare our hearts and lives in the ways we discussed.

FOLLOW-UP: Lead the children in beginning to prepare their hearts for Christmas by having a prayer and then baking cookies for a homebound person or homeless shelter.

16
The Courageous Shepherd Boy
Those Who Risk Their Lives for Others Are Heroes

SCRIPTURES: John 10:11; 15:13 GNT

OBJECT FOR SHARING: A religious statue, icon, or picture of a shepherd.

PRESENTATION: The story works well in Advent or near Christmas.

Who can tell us what a shepherd is? Have you ever thought about what it would be like to be a shepherd living out in the wilderness? Do you think you would ever be afraid of the dangers that are present in the wilderness?

Once upon a time, long, long ago, in a country far, far away, there was a group of shepherd boys living out in the wilderness taking care of their sheep. As the shepherds were counting their sheep, like they did every day, they found that one of them was missing. "Oh no, one of the sheep must have wandered off into the wilderness," one of the shepherd boys said.

"One of us must go look for it," another one replied. "Who will it be?"

Jeremias, a kind and compassionate young man, said, "I will go look for it." And so off into the wilderness he went with his rod and staff in hand.

Well, at times the path grew dark, and Jeremias was a little afraid. Because out in the wilderness one never knows what might be hiding behind the rocks or in the bushes—a snake curled up ready to strike, or a thief looking to rob or to steal, or a wild animal ready to devour some dinner.

Finally Jeremias rounded a turn in the path and in the distance he saw the lost sheep. "Oh no!" Jeremias cried, "my sheep, my sheep!" Getting ready to pounce on his sheep was a ferocious lion. "Get away from my sheep! Get away from my sheep!" Jeremias cried as he started running down the path, shaking his rod in the air. All of a sudden the lion turned on him, lurching right at his throat. Jeremias had risked his life for the good of his sheep.

Well, because of the sacrifice of Jeremias, the lost sheep was saved. She was able to run back to the flock where the other shepherds took her in their arms and cared for her until she was strong again. But there was no sign of Jeremias. Of course, all the other shepherd boys feared the worst.

But then, three days later they spied Jeremias coming in the distance. Though he had been injured by the lion and had been very weak for three days, he had been able to overcome the lion and drive him back into the wilderness. The other shepherd boys, and the sheep as well, received Jeremias with great joy. Jeremias had shown great courage. And he had risked his own life for the good of another.

That's what people sometimes do—risk their lives so that others might live better. There's a word for people like that—we call them heroes.

FOLLOW-UP: Lead the children in discussion of other professions in which people risk their lives for the well-being of others. Note if the children pick up on the connection between the shepherd boy and Jesus, the Good Shepherd.

17
I Spy
We Need to Be Alert, Observant to Spiritual Lessons Around Us

SCRIPTURE: Luke 2:27–32 GNT

OBJECTS FOR SHARING: Any objects in the room or worship space that might not be readily observed but that hold significance.

PRESENTATION: This story works best during Advent, though it could be adapted for any time. Scan the room or worship space ahead of time and choose two or three objects that the children can spot that they might not otherwise notice.

Perhaps you have heard of the game called "I spy." If so, then you know that the person who is "It" secretly spies something in the room and then says to everyone else something like, "I spy something green" or "I spy something round." Then everyone else starts guessing what the object is. You want to try it a couple of times? Okay, I spy something green (or whatever color or shape is best; give time for guesses). Good! You found it. Let's do it again—"I spy something round" (again give time for guesses). Great!

If we had time, the one who is first to guess the special object would be "It" and we would play the game until everyone got tired. But since we are limited for time, we best get to the point. What do you think the "I spy" game teaches us? Right. It teaches us to be alert, to be observant, to have our eyes open to see things around us that we might not otherwise see.

That's sort of what the season of Advent is about—being alert, observant, and having our eyes open to the spiritual meaning of this season. Advent is about looking for the blessings of God and seeing "God lessons" that we might not otherwise see. The Bible tells us about an elderly man who was watching for the baby Jesus to be born. He was looking carefully, so when Jesus' parents brought him to the Temple to be dedicated to God, Simeon spied him immediately because he was alert, observant, and looking for him.

In the weeks before Christmas it is easy to get caught up in all the hectic activities like decorating, running to the mall or shopping center, wrapping gifts, having Christmas parties, and so forth, so that we forget to think about the real reasons of the season. Advent teaches us to keep our eyes open so that we can "spy" the spiritual lessons of the season, what God might be trying to say to us.

FOLLOW-UP: Explore with the children ways that God, the Sacred, or Divinity might be revealed to them during this season and in their everyday lives.

18
The Good Shepherd
The Good News of God Is for Everyone

SCRIPTURE: Luke 2:8–12 GNT

OBJECT FOR SHARING: A statue, figurine, or picture of a shepherd.

PRESENTATION: This story works well during Advent when Luke's Christmas story is told, or on another Sunday of the year when Psalm 23 is included in the service.

What comes to mind when you hear the word "shepherds"? (*Give a moment for responses, which could include David the shepherd boy, Jesus the Good Shepherd, etc.*) Usually when we think of shepherds, we think of *good* shepherds, don't we?

But you know, not all shepherds were good. Sometimes shepherds could also be bad. What do you think would make one a *bad* shepherd? That is correct. A bad shepherd could let the sheep wander off and not try to find them. Or a bad shepherd could see a sheep caught in briars or underbrush and just leave it there. Since the sheep often belonged to someone else, the shepherd could steal the sheep and claim that a wild animal ate it. There were many ways that a shepherd could turn bad. For that reason, sometimes shepherds did not have a good reputation. The job of being a shepherd was sometimes thought of as one of the lowest jobs one could have, sort of like being a tax collector.

So it is interesting that when Luke tells the story of Jesus' birth, he tells us about the shepherds who visited the baby Jesus in the manger. Now, if shepherds did not always have a good reputation, why do you suppose Luke wanted us to know that the shepherds were the first ones to hear the news and go to the manger? I think it is because Luke wanted to be sure that we all know that God's good news about Jesus is for *everyone*. No one is left out, not even lowly shepherds.

When Jesus got older, he called himself the Good Shepherd. As the Good Shepherd, Jesus welcomes everyone.

So no matter who we are, or what our job in life is, or even what others might think about us, God loves us and wants us to be a part of the family of Jesus. And that's good news for each and every one of us!

FOLLOW-UP: Share and compare the two Christmas stories (Luke 2 and Matthew 2). Discuss with the children why Luke included the shepherds in his story whereas Matthew included kings (hint: Luke portrays Jesus as friend of the lowly and downtrodden, whereas Matthew portrays Jesus as the new King of the Jews).

19
Peacemakers
All of Us Are Called to
Work for Peace in Our Lives

SCRIPTURES: Matthew 5:9 GNT; Romans 14:19 GNT

OBJECT FOR SHARING: A police officer's badge.

PRESENTATION: If there is a police officer in the congregation, she or he might help with the lesson.

Good morning! Have you ever seen one of these? Do you know what it is? Right, it is a police officer's badge. Have any of you ever met a police officer? Do any of you know a police officer? What does a police officer do? A primary duty of the police officer is to help keep the peace. After all, sometimes police officers are referred to as "peace officers."

Let's imagine there is a rowdy group of people next door who hold a noisy party way into the night with blasting music, shouting, breaking of bottles, foul language, and fighting. What would the neighbors do in such a situation? They would likely call the police—peace officers—who would come to help restore the peace. Police officers as keepers of the peace perform a wonderful service for our communities. Life would be a lot more difficult without them.

As people of faith, we are also called to be peacemakers, to bring peace to our troubled world. In fact, this time of year we think about the coming of the Prince of Peace, whose example calls us to make peace in the world as well.

What can all of us do to make peace in our homes and communities? Some steps that lead to peace in our daily lives include loving others as we want to be loved, forgiving others, doing to others as we want them to do unto us, and seeking to be gentle, kind, and caring.

Can you think of any objects that stand for peace? How about the dove, or the peace lily? Whenever we see doves or peace lilies, they can be reminders that each of us is called to be a peacemaker. Likewise, when we see a police officer, it can remind us that we, too, are called to work for peace. And we can always remember what Jesus said: "Blessed [happy] are the peacemakers, for they shall be called children of God."

FOLLOW-UP: 1) Let a police officer lead the children in discovering ways that they can help make peace in the community and world.
2) Lead the children in placing a Peace Lily somewhere in the building in a prominent place as a reminder to all that we are to be makers of peace.

20

So Many Days on the Calendar
We Live by Taking One Day at a Time

SCRIPTURE: Matthew 6:31–34 GNT

OBJECT FOR SHARING: A new nature calendar that can be held up for everyone to see.

PRESENTATION: This lesson works best on the first Sunday of the New Year.

One of the things that I like best about this time of year is getting a new calendar. The calendars that I like best have nature pictures—a different picture for each month of the year. I find it relaxing to look at pictures of beautiful waterfalls, majestic mountains, colorful flowers, soaring birds, and the like.

But when I fan through the pages of a new calendar and see all the days of the upcoming year, sometimes it almost overwhelms me. All of those days—365 in all—with all the things I will have to do on those days! Think of all the work that has to be done, all the problems that are to be solved, all the places there will be to go. It sort of makes your brain feel like it is going to explode, doesn't it?

But you know what? We are not expected to think about all the days of the coming year, with all the work that is to be done, and all the problems that are to be solved, and with all the places we will have to go. We remember something that Jesus taught about this very thing. Jesus said, "Do not worry about tomorrow.... There is no need to add to the troubles each day brings" (Matt. 6:34 GNT). In other words, we can only live life one day at a time. We should only be concerned about living *today*, *this day*, and doing the best we can to live this day to the fullest. We cannot change anything about tomorrow or next week by worrying about it. But we can pray and ask God to guide us and help us to live this day and do what we need to do.

So, as we hang up those new calendars for the New Year, let's not worry about the 364 days that come after today. We cannot mark off a day until it comes, can we? Instead, let's try to focus on the beautiful and relaxing picture that each month brings and let those pictures remind us that the God of creation helps us to live one day at a time.

FOLLOW-UP: If possible, give each child a beautiful nature calendar as discussed in the lesson. Such inexpensive calendars can sometimes be found at discount or "dollar" stores.

21
Following a Star
Sometimes Good Things Take Effort

SCRIPTURE: Matthew 2:1–2 GNT

OBJECT FOR SHARING: Icon, statue, or other picture of the Magi.

PRESENTATION: This story works best on the Sunday nearest Epiphany, January 6. Hold the icon or picture until the end of the story to foster suspense in the beginning.

"Do you see that?" Melchoir yelled across the room to his companions.

"See what?" Balthazar replied, almost jumping off his stool.

"There, in the sky. That new star," Melchoir exclaimed. "Right over there." He pointed with outstretched arm.

"Yes, I see it," Kaspar joyfully said. "It is a new star."

"Yes, I see it now, too," Balthazar yelled with delight.

"You know what that means," Melchoir told them. "It means a new king has been born."

"A new king. How exciting!" Kaspar said.

"Hey, I have an idea: let's follow the star and see where it leads us," Melchoir suggested.

"But where do you think it would take us?" Balthazar asked. He wasn't so sure.

"I don't know," Melchoir said, "but does it really matter? Wherever it leads us will be worth the journey."

"Ah, I don't know," Balthazar protested. "It could be a long, cold, tiresome journey. There could be storms and bandits and wild animals."

"Yes, but there could also be beautiful cities and palaces and a new king. Yes, a new king!" Kaspar exclaimed. He was also getting excited about the possibilities.

"But what, what if we get lost, or run out of food, or our camels run away?" Balthazar continued to protest.

"Balthazar, Balthazar," Melchoir said, trying to calm his fears. We won't get lost, because we will keep our eyes on the star and it will lead us. We will take plenty of food for the journey. And we'll even take extra camels in case we lose some. And besides all of that, the Creator of the world will protect us."

Kaspar agreed.

"You know," the wise old Balthazar explained, "good things almost always require hard work and sacrifice. And it is important that we search for the truth until we find it. And when God sends us a star to follow, when God sends us a sign, we need to follow it."

After much preparations and planning, that is just what Melchoir, Kaspar, and Balthazar did. They set out on a long, hard journey. They went in search of the truth. They followed the star, the sign, that God gave them. And finally—at last!—they came to where the star rested and they found what they were looking for: the newborn King of the world. And their lives were changed forever.

FOLLOW-UP: Lead the children, at night if possible, in studying the sky. A field trip to a planetarium would be a nice treat.

22
Elephant In the Room
Problems Should Be
Addressed,
Not Ignored

SCRIPTURES: Matthew 18:15 GNT; Ephesians 4:15 GNT

OBJECT FOR SHARING: A picture of an elephant.

PRESENTATION: Use on or near Christian Unity Sunday, or any other time when it seems relevant.

What would you do if you were to get up from sleep one morning and come into the living room to find an elephant standing there? (*Allow time for answers.*) Most of us would say something, wouldn't we? Something like, "Mom, Dad, there's an elephant in the living room!" You wouldn't just ignore it, would you? Of course not! How silly.

Some self-help groups talk about the elephant in the room. What they mean by that is there is a problem—a *big* problem that everybody sees, but nobody wants to talk about it. Everybody just tries to ignore it and pretend that it doesn't exist. If everybody ignores the problem—the elephant in the room—then hopefully it will just go away on its own.

But you know what? Many, if not most, problems that are ignored don't just go away. Often they just keep getting bigger and bigger, like a growing baby elephant.

Perhaps that is why Jesus instructed his followers not to ignore the elephant in the room. Jesus didn't talk about elephants. But he did talk about problems and about when people do things to hurt us. And what Jesus said was when someone does something that makes us angry or hurts our feelings, we shouldn't just try to ignore it. And we shouldn't go and talk to someone else about it. The best thing to do is to go to that person and say, "You know, that thing that you did or that thing that you said upset me or hurt my feelings." And we should do it in a compassionate way, in such a way that we restore the relationship that might otherwise be broken. By going to the other person and saying in a very kind and loving manner, "That thing that you did hurt my feelings, so can we talk about it?" we can make life a lot better for everyone.

So, someday if you find that there is an elephant in your room—that is, if you find there is a big problem with a friend at school or someone in your family—I hope you won't try to ignore it. Because when we try to ignore the problem it usually won't go away. But when we talk about the problem in the spirit of love, then we might just find a way to make the problem go away.

FOLLOW-UP: Lead the children in role playing, taking turns speaking to one another about fabricated scenarios such as stealing a bike, failing to send a birthday card, and the like.

23
Sun and Moon
Like the Moon, We Can
Reflect the Light of God

SCRIPTURES: John 1:8-9 GNT; Matthew 5:14 GNT

OBJECT FOR SHARING: A round rock that can resemble the moon and a small flashlight and mirror.

PRESENTATION: This story works best during Advent or Epiphany when the church is focusing on light. With some adaptation it could be used near the winter solstice. Line up someone beforehand to hold either the mirror or the flashlight, positioning that person to reflect light on a certain spot in the worship space.

What is the brightest light in our sky? The sun, good! What is it about the sun that causes it to give off light? Right. The sun is a giant ball of gas that burns all the time. The burning gas—sort of like the gas stoves that many of us use to cook our food—gives off both light and heat.

Now, what is the second brightest light in our sky? Right again! The moon. The moon gives off light in the same way that the sun does, right—burning gas? No, the moon is a totally different kind of creation. The moon is nothing but a big ball of rock for the most part. If that is so, then how does the moon give off light? The moon merely reflects the light given off by the sun, much like this mirror reflects the light given off by this flashlight (*demonstration*).

Now, what does this science lesson have to do with faith? Well, a long, long time ago a man named John came preaching in the wilderness about a light from God. John said he was not the light itself, but rather, he was merely a reflection of the true light. And who do Christians believe the Light of the world was, and is? Right, Jesus.

Perhaps this is what Jesus meant when he said to all who follow his teachings, "You are the light of the world." Like the moon, and like John, we are meant to reflect the light and love of God as revealed in Jesus.

FOLLOW-UP: Let the children take turns "being the light" by holding the flashlight and "reflecting the light" by holding the mirror. Then discuss different ways that each of us can be much-needed light to the world.

24
Who Can Be a Poet?
All of Us Are Free to Write Poetry and Express Ourselves

SCRIPTURES: Exodus 15:20-21 GNT; Psalm 45:1 GNT

OBJECT FOR SHARING: A picture of poet Phillis Wheatley, which can be found at http://darkwing.uoregon.edu/~rbear/ wheatley.html.

PRESENTATION: This story works well on or near Martin Luther King Jr. Day.

Can anyone tell us what a poem is? A poem is a collection of words, each of which is chosen very carefully, that expresses an experience, idea, or emotion. Often the words in a poem rhyme—"the cat in the hat," for example. And often the words have a rhythm that you can hear, such as, "The *years* have *come* and *gone* so soon."

One of the oldest poems in the Bible is the Song of Miriam, a poem that Miriam, Moses' sister, wrote after God had delivered the Hebrew people from bondage and slavery.

Can you write a poem? I can write a poem. I bet you can, too. Here are a couple of lines of poetry that I have written (*at this point read a few lines of poetry or verse that you or someone in the congregation has written*). Every one of us here today is free to write down in poetry or verse what we are thinking, feeling, or experiencing.

But there was a time when just anyone could not write poetry. Some people, because of their race or station in life, were forbidden from reading and writing.

That is why Phyllis Wheatley is so important to everyone who likes poetry. Ms. Wheatley was an African American who was born in 1753 or 1754 and captured and brought to America to be sold as a slave. The Wheatley family, who lived in Boston, Massachusetts, bought Phyllis and took her home. The Wheatleys were members of the Old South Congregational Church in Boston, and Phyllis became a member there, too.

John and Susanna Wheatley were different from most slave owners of that time. Most slave owners forbade their slaves from learning to read and write. But the Wheatleys actually encouraged young Phyllis to learn, and they taught her English, Latin, history, and literature. Phyllis soon learned that she loved to write. So by the age of eleven or so, she started writing poetry. By the time Phyllis was fourteen years old, her first poem already had been published. And by the time she was twenty, she had published a complete book of poetry. So, you see, for those who like poetry, Phyllis Wheatley is important because she was the first published African American poet.

Here are a few of Wheatley's lines from her poem titled "Thoughts on the *Works of Providence*":

> Infinite *Love* where'er we turn our eyes
> Appears: this ev'ry creature's wants supplies;
> This most is heard in *Nature's* constant voice,
> This makes the morn, and this the eve rejoice;
> This bids the fost'ring rains and dews descend
> To nourish all, to serve one gen'ral end,
> The good of man: yet man ungrateful pays
> But little homage, and but little praise.
> To him, whose works arry'd with mercy shine,
> What songs should rise, how constant, how divine!

Wheatly's language is not like what people write today, this is true. Nevertheless, Phyllis Wheatley is an inspiration to all of us. If Phyllis, who was a slave, could study, learn, and write as she did, just think of what we who are free to do anything we want to can accomplish, if we set our minds to it.

FOLLOW-UP: 1) Lead the children in writing a couple verses of simple poetry based on their feelings, ideas, or observations of the natural world. 2) If children are old enough, explain haiku poetry (three unrhymed lines consisting of five, seven, and five syllables respectively).

25

God's Special Hiding Place[4]

God's Presence Is in Each Heart

SCRIPTURES: Ezekiel 36:26–27 GNT; Romans 5:5 GNT

OBJECT FOR SHARING: A heart, perhaps a heart-shaped candy box, available at Valentine's Day.

PRESENTATION: This lesson works well on the Sunday prior to Valentine's Day. Inside the box place a symbol of God's Spirit, such as a picture of a flame or a dove.

The story goes that a long, long time ago, soon after God had finished creating the earth, God decided to hide somewhere in the creation that had been made. As God was wondering about how to do this, all the angels gathered around.

"Why don't you hide yourself deep in the earth?" one of the angels said.

God thought for awhile and then said, "No, it won't be long before men and women will learn how to mine the treasures of the earth. I need to find a place where I won't be found too quickly, because in their long searching for me my creatures will grow in spirit and understanding."

"Well, why don't you hide yourself in the ocean?" another angel suggested.

"No, that won't work either," God said, "because men and women will soon explore the ocean and find all that is hidden there."

The angels thought and thought. Finally a third angel said, "Why don't you hide yourself in the human heart? They will never think of looking there."

"That's it!" God said. "That is the perfect hiding place."

And so it is that God secretly hides in every human heart of every baby that is born and stays hidden there until that person grows enough in spirit and understanding to find God deep within. And when that happens, everyone who finds God there in her or his heart has fellowship with God for all eternity.

FOLLOW-UP: Question for discussion: How do you think we know when we have found God in our hearts? (Answer: When we live in love with God and others, loving God with all our heart, soul, mind, and strength, and our neighbor as ourself.)

26
Not Like You
Each of Us Is to Be the Person We Were Created to Be

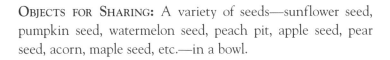

Scripture: Galatians 6:4 GNT

Objects for Sharing: A variety of seeds—sunflower seed, pumpkin seed, watermelon seed, peach pit, apple seed, pear seed, acorn, maple seed, etc.—in a bowl.

Presentation: This lesson works well when the service theme is diversity or inclusivity.

Good morning! I have brought with me today a variety of seeds. *(Allow each child to take one seed from the container).* Now, hold up your seed. What do you notice as you look at everyone's seeds? All of them are different, aren't they. No two are exactly alike.

Let's think a minute. If I plant an acorn (we'll call it an oak seed), can I expect an apple tree to grow? Of course not. If I plant an apple seed, can I expect a peach tree to grow? Of course not. An acorn is meant to grow an oak tree, and an apple seed is meant to grow an apple tree, and a peach pit (seed) is meant to grow a peach tree. That's the way God planned it.

And the apple tree should not make fun of the peach tree because it is not an apple tree, and the oak tree should not make fun of the maple tree because it is not an oak tree.

Now, turn and look at each other. Do any of you look exactly alike? Of course not. If there were identical twins here, they might look almost the same. But even identical twins would be different in some ways. The point I am trying to make is that each one of us was created to be something different. It's almost like each of us has a certain kind of seed inside of us that is to grow into the person we were created to be.

Now what this means is that God doesn't expect Ben to be Jack. And God doesn't expect Jack to be Matt. And God doesn't expect Catherine to be Summer. And God doesn't expect Summer to be Pastor Hammer.

No, God wants Ben to be Ben, Jack to be Jack, Matt to be Matt, Catherine to be Catherine, and Summer to be Summer!

God wants each of us to be the person that we are inside, the person we were created to be. Just as God doesn't expect a peach seed to grow an apple tree, God doesn't expect us to be somebody else, somebody we are not. God wants us to be proud of the person we were created to be.

The joy for each of us is to discover and to become the kind of person we have been created to be.

FOLLOW-UP: Lead the children in examining and discussing the various seeds, paying special attention to color, feel, smell, and relation of the size of the seed to the size of the fruit, vegetable, or tree it produces. Then lead them in planting the seeds so that in future weeks they can see how some of them grow.

27
Invite FRANC to Church
All of Us Know Persons
We Can Invite to Church

SCRIPTURE: John 1:35–37, 40–42a GNT

OBJECTS FOR SHARING: Small index cards to be shared at the end of the lesson that might look something like this:

Invite to church:
F riends
R elatives
A cquaintances
N eighbors
C lub members

PRESENTATION: This lesson will work on a Sunday when the theme is evangelism or outreach, or for a special "Friend Day," when churchgoers invite their friends to visit. The lesson might be printed on a flip chart or prepared as a Power Point presentation.

Who knows FRANC? What do you suppose FRANC looks like?

Well, actually FRANC is an acronym. Say that with me—AK-ra-nim. Does anyone know what an acronym is?

An acronym is a word in which every letter is the first letter of another word. The first letter of each word is combined to make one word out of all the words.

So in FRANC, the letter "F" stand for friends.

The letter "R" stands for relatives.

The letter "A" stands for acquaintances, people we see every now and then, such as our dentist or the person who cuts our hair.

Can anyone guess what the letter "N" stands for? That's right— Neighbors.

And then there is the letter "C," which stands for club members. In the case of adults the "C" can also stand for coworkers.

So, when we put all the first letters of friends, relatives, acquaintances, neighbors, and club members together, we come up with the name FRANC.

As we read the stories of the early followers of Jesus, we see that they were very excited about inviting their friends, relatives, acquaintances, neighbors, and club members and coworkers to their church services. The gospel of John tells how Andrew invited his brother, Peter, to come meet Jesus. Because of Andrew's invitation, Peter eventually became one of the most important leaders in the early church.

Inviting others to come meet Jesus is something that every one of us can do, too. For all of us have friends, neighbors, relatives, acquaintances, and maybe even club members or coworkers who would love to come to a wonderful church like ours—if they only knew about it. But if we don't invite them, they may never know. It is our joy to tell them!

FOLLOW-UP: Lead the children in writing down, on the back of the FRANC index cards, the first name of a friend, relative, acquaintance, neighbor, and club member that they might invite to church.

28
A Special Kind of Book
We Can Often Turn Problems into Opportunities for Blessing

SCRIPTURE: Genesis 50:15, 19–20 GNT

OBJECT FOR SHARING: Sample of Braille text.

PRESENTATION: In the beginning, invite the children to close their eyes and let you run their fingers over the Braille, seeing if they can identify what their fingers are feeling. If someone is available who is familiar with Braille or has taught persons who are blind, invite that person to join you and share some insight.

About two hundred years ago, in the country of France, there was a little boy named Louis. At the age of three, Louis became blind; he could no longer see.

Now, way back then some people thought that persons who were blind or deaf were not able to learn, so often they didn't get to go to school. But little Louis did get to go to school, a special school that someone started for children like himself who were blind. And he proved himself to be very smart, especially in science and music. Louis, though blind himself, became a teacher for the other students who were also blind.

Then at the age of nineteen or so, Louis came up with the idea of using dots on a page of paper to make a special kind of writing for blind people. Dots are punched in the back of a piece of paper so they are raised up on the front side. There are six dots to each little square called a cell. The way the dots are arranged determines which letter of the alphabet or number those six dots stand for. Persons who are blind learn to run their fingers over the dots and read the words that have been formed by the dots.

Does anyone know what Louis's full name was? It was Louis Braille. And his system of writing for the blind is called the Braille System.

But wait, there's more! A few years later, another man by the name of Samuel Gridley Howe went from America to France and England to see how those who were blind and deaf were being educated. It was on this trip that Howe learned about the Braille System and brought it back to the Perkins School for the Blind in Boston, Massachusetts. It was at the Perkins School for the Blind where another famous American would be educated. Does anyone know who that was? It was Helen Keller. Keller also became a teacher and inspiration to millions.

One of the great lessons that Louis, Samuel, and Helen teach us is that whenever we have a problem, we also have an opportunity to find a solution for that problem that will not only make life better for ourselves, but maybe better for others as well. That is what Joseph did. With trust in God, Joseph turned his problem of being sold into slavery by his brothers into an opportunity to bring about much good for the world. Indeed, as they say, problems are just opportunities in disguise!

FOLLOW-UP: 1) Lead the children (with help from someone who is familiar with Braille) in punching dots in a piece of paper to spell out their names. 2) Discuss places where Braille might be seen (such as on public doors, elevators, etc.), as well as things each of us can do to be more sensitive to persons who are sight impaired. 3) Tell the story of Joseph (Genesis 37–50), how he was sold into slavery, imprisoned in Egypt, rose to prominence, and later saved his family from starvation.

29
A Rock in My Shoe
Like Rocks in Our Shoes, Feelings Trouble Us Until We Lose Them

SCRIPTURE: Hebrews 13:18 GNT

OBJECT FOR SHARING: A small pebble that has been placed in one's shoe just prior to the story.

PRESENTATION: This lesson works well during Lent, when our focus is on spiritual self-improvement.

Have you ever had a rock in your shoe? Most of us have at one time or another. *(Sit down in front of the children, remove a shoe, and shake out a small pebble.)* You know, in the past when I have gotten a small pebble in my shoe I have sometimes tried to ignore it. I just kept walking thinking that if I ignored it long enough, it would go away, maybe shift to one side of my shoe and not bother me any more, or maybe miraculously disappear altogether. You see, I didn't want to take time to sit down and untie my shoe, shake out the rock, then put my shoe back on and tie it again. Or maybe there wasn't a good place to sit down. At any rate, I just kept hoping that if I ignored the pebble long enough it would go away and stop irritating me. But you know what? Sooner or later I had to sit down, untie my shoe, shake out the rock, and then tie my shoe again.

You know, I have been thinking how feelings that we have inside our hearts and our heads are like that. Sometimes we have feelings that irritate us. They may be feelings of anger because someone has done something to hurt or upset us. They may be feelings of guilt over something we did that we know is wrong. They may be feelings of sadness because we have changed classes at school and lost a teacher we really loved. Sometimes we tend to think that if we just ignore these kinds of feelings—like a rock in our shoe—long enough, they will go way. Sometimes they might go away, but most times we need to take time to deal with those feelings. We need to sit down with the person we are angry at, or with the person we have wronged, or with a parent or teacher or someone else and tell them about those feelings inside that are irritating us. And after we talk with someone about those irritating feelings, we will often feel much, much better, just like we do when we take time to get the rock out of our shoe. There's nothing quite like a clear conscience to make us feel better.

(*Replacing shoe*) Yes, that feels a whole lot better.

FOLLOW-UP: Through artwork, encourage the children to create a feeling they are holding inside that is irritating them. Then give one-on-one opportunity for those who wish to do so to share their artwork and its meaning.

30
A Special Place
Everyone Needs a Special Place That Renews the Mind

SCRIPTURE: Luke 22:39–41 GNT

OBJECTS FOR SHARING: Any number of objects—religious or personal—that help bring calm to the soul.

PRESENTATION: Perhaps a sample "special place" can be created in the worship space by including a chair, small table, or lamp where the objects can be arranged to bring the lesson to life.

Good morning! I have brought some things with me this morning. But before we talk about them, I have a question for you. And the question is this: Do you have a place in your home—perhaps a small space in your bedroom, or a corner in the living room or den, or maybe a small space in the basement—that you can make your own very special place? A place where you can go and think? A place where you can go and restore your mind? A place where you can go to feel peaceful again?

It is important that every one of us—no matter how young or how old we are—have such a place. Because every now and then, all of us need to go to a place where we can be alone with just our thoughts, a place that relaxes us, a place that rests our minds, a place that makes us feel peaceful again.

Jesus had a special place where he often went to relax, pray, and feel peaceful again. It was an olive garden, called the Garden of Gethsemane.

At our special place, we may have some objects that help us to relax and return to a state of peace. It might be a religious object such as a wood carving of someone praying. Or a carving of St. Francis, who worked for peace and gave us the peace prayer. Or a Bible or other special book that helps us to relax and feel peaceful again. Or even a picture, such as a scenic calendar, that relaxes the mind and makes one feel peaceful.

One of the best things that I have found to have in my workspace to help me stay relaxed and return to peace is a nature calendar that has a different picture for every month of the year. As I reflect upon beautiful scenes of nature, the changing of the seasons, and how God works in the different seasons of the year, I feel better inside—more calm and peaceful.

The objects that you pick for your special place probably would be different than mine, because each one of us is different and has different likes and interests. Can you think of some other things that you might have in your special spot to help you relax and feel peaceful again? (*Give time for answers, some of which might include a rock, seashell, photo of a loved one, flowers, pressed leaves, cross, stuffed animal, spiritual journal, or CD player.*)

The important thing is not what we have in our space, but that we do have such a space where we can retreat to and be restored and made peaceful again.

FOLLOW-UP: Continue discussing with the children different objects that might be used to decorate one's special place. Explore with them the benefits—to oneself, one's family, the community, and the world—when one's mind is peaceful as opposed to fretful and agitated.

31
A Special Parade
Children Can Honor Christ in Many Ways

<small>SCRIPTURE:</small> Luke 19:37–38 GNT

<small>OBJECTS FOR SHARING:</small> Palm branches and robe, coat, or cloak.

<small>PRESENTATION:</small> This story is designed for Palm Sunday, the Sunday before Easter. Before beginning, dramatically open the robe, coat, or cloak and spread it out on the floor in the aisle or walkway in front of the children. Then lay down some palm branches around it.

What do you suppose it would have been like to have been in Jerusalem about 1,975 years ago today? Well, maybe it would have been something like this:

It was to be a special day. (*Insert some of children's name*) were excited. A parade was coming. Jesus, the great prophet, was riding into town.

Finally the children could see in the distance a crowd coming down the dirt road on the hill. In the middle of the crowd was a man riding on a donkey. As the crowd got closer, the children could hear the people shouting: "Hosanna! Blessed is the one who comes in the name of God! Hosanna in the highest!"

But then the children saw something they thought was kind of strange. People started taking off their coats and spreading them out on the ground in front of the man on the donkey. When the children saw their parents take off their coats and spread them on the roadway, they decided to do the same. So very quickly *(insert children's names)* removed their coats and very carefully spread them on the dirt road just in time for the prophet Jesus to pass over them.

After the crowd had passed, everyone started picking up their coats, dusting them off, and putting them back on.

"Look! My coat is all dirty," one of the children cried to another.

"Yes, mine is too," a second child replied.

"Mother, why did we do that?"

"Do what?" The mother replied.

"Take our coats off so the man on the donkey could walk over them and get them all dirty?"

"Well, because the man on the donkey is not just a prophet. He is a king—God's new king," the mother replied. "Taking off your coat to a king is a way of showing honor, letting the king know you think he is special."

The children thought about what they had seen and heard.

"A king! My coat was run over by a king!" one of the children happily exclaimed.

"Mine too!" cried another, and another, and another. The children again looked at the dirt on their coats, but this time the dirt didn't bother them at all. In fact, it seemed special. It is sort of nice, they thought, to share what you have in order to honor the King.

FOLLOW-UP: 1) Encourage the children to find pictures of Jerusalem and the Mount of Olives where the triumphal entry occurred. 2) Ask them to use their imaginations to think of tangible ways we can honor Christ the King today.

32
Full or Empty?
The Empty Egg Symbolizes the Empty Tomb

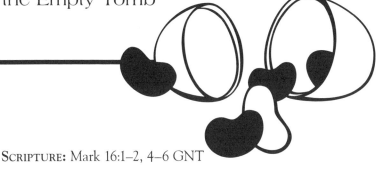

SCRIPTURE: Mark 16:1–2, 4–6 GNT

OBJECT FOR SHARING: A basket of plastic Easter eggs, all filled with candy of your choosing except one special one that is empty.

PRESENTATION: Of course, this story is for Easter Sunday, or perhaps the Sunday after.

Good morning! Which do you think is better? Full *(hold up and shake a plastic egg filled with candy)* or empty *(hold up and shake an empty plastic egg)*? Better here *(again shake full egg)* or better here *(again shake empty egg)*? We are conditioned or trained to believe that the full egg is better, aren't we? Why do you think so? Right. Plastic eggs are associated with candy inside.

In reality, however, on Easter empty is actually better *(take apart and hold up an empty egg)*. Can anyone tell us why? Correct. It is because the *empty* egg reminds us of the empty tomb. Who can tell us what a *tomb* is? A tomb is a little cave carved in the earth as a place to bury the dead.

As we study the Easter story, we find that all of the good news of Easter started with the empty tomb. When Mary Magdalene and some of the other disciples went to the tomb of Jesus, where his body had been laid after he had been taken from the cross, they found it empty. "He is not here!" is the good news they heard. When Mary and Peter and John looked in the tomb, they found it to be so. Jesus was not there. The story says that the strips of cloth that had been wound around his body were piled up where Jesus had been laid, but he was nowhere to be found. And the empty tomb set off an entire chain of events in which the early followers of Jesus experienced him as being alive, raised from the dead.

So whenever you see an Easter egg, I hope that in addition to thinking about the candy that might be inside you will also remember that the empty egg reminds us of the empty tomb. And if it hadn't been for the empty tomb, we wouldn't be celebrating Easter at all.

FOLLOW-UP: 1) Encourage the children to research the history of the egg as it is associated with Easter. 2) Explore other Easter themes, such as the new life in the form of a baby chick breaking forth from real eggs as Jesus broke forth from the tomb in new life.

33
Eric's Baseball Glove
Alarm and Joy of Jesus' Disciples on Easter

SCRIPTURE: John 20:1–18 NRSV

OBJECTS FOR SHARING: An old and tattered baseball glove and a new one, if possible.

PRESENTATION: Use this story on Easter Sunday or one of the Sundays shortly thereafter, depending upon the lectionary readings of the day.

How many of you like to play baseball or softball? Well, Eric, a boy about your age, loved to play baseball, too. But Eric's baseball glove was an old, worn, somewhat ragged glove that his father had given him. Since it was the only baseball glove that Eric owned, he loved it very much. He cherished it more than anything else he owned. In fact, Eric's old, tattered baseball glove was his most prized possession. Every day after Eric finished playing baseball, he would take his baseball glove to his room and place it under the foot of his bed so he always knew where to find it.

Well, one day, when it was time to go to practice in preparation for the big game on Saturday, Eric went to his room, got down on his knees, and reached under the foot of his bed for his glove. But he could not find it. So he pulled up the bedspread and looked all around under the bed, but no glove was to be found.

Eric ran through the house crying, "My glove! My glove! I can't find my glove. It's gone." Tears were running down his face. He was very upset. Finally Eric found his mom. "Mom, my glove is gone! My glove is gone!" he panted.

Eric's mom put her arm on his shoulder, and with a smile said, "Eric, why are you crying?"

"Because my baseball glove is gone. It's not where I keep it."

"Have you looked in the closet?" his mother asked.

"No, I never put it in the closet. Why would my glove be in the closet?"

"Just go and see," his mother assured him.

Wiping tears from the corners of his eyes, Eric did as his mother said. He went to his room and opened to the closet door. And there hanging in front of his eyes was a brand new baseball glove unlike any he had ever seen before. It was beautiful! Eric pulled the new glove close to his heart. He was so happy, but he just couldn't believe it. Though his old glove was gone, the new glove that he now had to take its place was so much better. And he could learn to love the new glove even more than the old one.

Now, there is an Easter lesson in this story for us. For the first Christian disciples, Jesus was what they loved and cherished more than anything else in the world. But then Jesus was crucified and buried in a stone cave. When they went to the cave on that first Easter morning to finish his burial, what did they find? That's right—nothing. The tomb was empty. So they were upset, and crying. Mary went running down the path crying, "He's gone! He's gone! I can't find Jesus!"

But then Mary and the other disciples experienced Jesus to be alive, but in a new and much better way. They were so happy! Though the Jesus they came to know after Easter was different from the one they knew before, they learned to love him even more.

FOLLOW-UP: Invite the children to share stories of times when they lost something and then were filled with joy when they found it again.

34
Keeping a Proper Focus
It Is Important to Stay Focused on Jesus

Scripture: Hebrews 12:2 GNT

Object for Sharing: A small picture of Jesus, which can be found in a children's Bible or Bible picture storybook, and a magnifying glass.

Presentation: Use this story on Ascension Sunday, when the gospel or Acts reading is about the disciples, whose focus was up in the clouds, or on a Sunday when the church is thinking about those with disabilities, especially visual disabilities.

Who can tell us what it means to focus? To focus is to adjust our eyes or our vision so that we can see more clearly. What kinds of things might we need to focus? Binoculars, telescope, microscope, a magnifying glass—those all are good answers.

Let's go with the magnifying glass, because I just happen to have one with me this morning. Let's suppose that while looking at Bible storybook we were to find a picture of Jesus, and that there was something in that picture that we wanted to get a better look at. I just happen to have a small picture of Jesus with me today as well. Now, can I just hold the magnifying glass anywhere I want to see the picture more clearly? (*Hold magnifying glass at a distance so the picture is fuzzy).* Well, at first you might think so. But actually, the magnifying glass has to be moved so that it is at just the right distance from the picture to make it clear. But if we hold the magnifying glass at just the right distance away from the picture, we can see it much more clearly. In other words, we have focused.

When you come to think of it, isn't that what we should be doing every day of our lives—focusing upon Jesus, and his teachings? Keeping our eyes clearly upon Jesus and trying to see what he would have us do and how he would have us live? That's what being Jesus' followers is all about.

FOLLOW-UP: Discuss what the children might do to help those who are visually impaired.

35
Seeds of God
Biblical Teachings Are Like Seeds That Take Root and Grow in Our Lives

SCRIPTURE: Luke 8:11, 15 GNT

OBJECTS FOR SHARING: A children's Bible, with any variety of seeds that can be easily seen, such as pumpkin seeds, positioned on the page in Luke 8:4–15 so that they will slide out when the Bible is opened.

PRESENTATION: This story works well in the spring at planting time. At the beginning of the story, open the Bible in such a way that the children can easily see the seeds on the page.

Good morning! I have a special story for you today (*open the Bible*). Oops! Looks like some seeds fell out of the Bible. Why do you suppose that is?

Curiously enough, the story that I have selected for this morning is about seeds. I invite you to listen very carefully (*read Luke 8:4–15, preferably from a children's Bible such as the Contemporary English Version or Good News Translation*).

Just like seeds that are ready to fall into good soil and grow into beautiful flowers, tasty fruits, and healthy vegetables, the Bible is full of word seeds that are just waiting to take root in our hearts and grow into something beautiful in our lives. But in order for that to happen, we have to either read the word seeds or hear them read to us. That is why it is so important that each of us have a Bible that we can easily read and understand and why it is so important that we come to church as often as we can so the wonderful word seeds can fall upon our ears, sink deep into our hearts, and cause something beautiful to grow.

FOLLOW-UP: Lead the children in planting a variety of flower seeds in small planters or on the church property that can later be enjoyed by everyone.

36
A Special Tree
There Are Many Ways to Honor Others

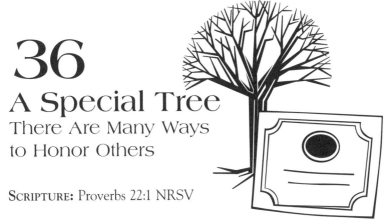

SCRIPTURE: Proverbs 22:1 NRSV

OBJECT FOR SHARING: A sample plaque that honors someone (many churches have several items donated in honor of someone that might be used as illustrations, or a plaque could be made of white card stock and a metal stake).

PRESENTATION: Brainstorm about the many ways people honor others: park benches, church pews, stained glass windows.

"Amanda, how about you help me with a little job this morning," Amanda's dad said just as they were finishing their Saturday morning breakfast.

"Do I *have* to?" Amanda said wearily. "Saturday is the only day I have to watch cartoons. Besides, I don't like to work."

"It won't take long," her dad assured. "And we'll have fun together, I promise."

Amanda rolled her eyes. "Oh, all right, if it won't take long."

A few minutes later Amanda and her dad were standing on the sidewalk near the street with two shovels, one for each of them. "Right here will be a good spot for our new tree," Amanda's dad said as he drew a circle on the ground with the point of his shovel. "Let's start digging." Amanda's dad showed her how to point the shovel in the dirt and place her foot on the shovel to exert pressure and push down. After a couple of digs, Amanda was finding shoveling to be quite fun and satisfying.

Fifteen minutes later, they stood before a round hole in the ground about as big as a beach ball. "Well, that should be big enough," Amanda's dad said. "Let's get the tree." He opened the back of the van, eased out a six-foot-tall tree and carried it to the hole. Carefully they positioned the tree in the hole so it was standing just right and filled in the hole with the loose dirt they had dug. Then they covered the soil with mulch and with the water hose gave it a good drink.

"Now, doesn't that look nice?" Amanda's dad quizzed. Amanda had to agree that it did. "But there's one more thing we have to do."

"Oh no, more work?" Amanda complained.

"Well, not really," her dad said as he pulled something from his back pocket. It was a small metal sign.

"What's that?" Amanda asked.

"Well, I'm glad you asked that," her dad replied. "This is an honorary plaque that shows that this tree was planted to honor someone who is very special. Every person who walks by this tree can read this sign and think good thoughts about the person whose name is on it."

Now Amanda was really curious. "Who does it honor?" she asked excitedly. "Whose name is on the plaque?"

"Well, why don't you read it for yourself?" her dad invited.

Amanda took the metal sign in her hand and read out-loud: "This tree has been planted *in honor of* Amanda Smith."

As Amanda's dad took the plaque and carefully placed it in the ground near the tree, she was proud—proud of her dad's love, proud she had learned to shovel, and proud that he had wanted to plant a tree in her honor.

FOLLOW-UP: Discuss the scripture verse (Prov. 22:1) that speaks of the importance of having a good name and how we honor the name of others by dedicating trees and other such things to them. Lead the children in planting a tree in honor of someone that everyone knows and loves.

37
Letting God Grow
The Divine Image in Us Needs to Be Nurtured

SCRIPTURES: Psalm 8:4–5 GNT; Ephesians 4:15 GNT

OBJECT FOR SHARING: An acorn (preferably) or other seed that has been planted in a terrarium jar and sprouted.

PRESENTATION: Use this lesson in the springtime or another day when the creation stories in the opening chapters of Genesis are the readings for the day.

Perhaps you have seen something similar to this before. It is called a terrarium. Sometimes a terrarium like this one can occur naturally when a bottle is thrown out on the ground (something we would not want to do) and soil and a seed wash into it. Then when the warm sunlight shines on the bottle, the heat causes the seed to sprout and grow. Everything a seed needs to sprout and grow is contained inside the bottle—moisture and soil that contains nutrients.

Now, it appears that we may soon have a problem. Can anyone tell me what that problem is? Correct. Soon the plant is going to outgrow the bottle that contains it. Unless the plant can be removed and planted outdoors, it might die.

Letting God Grow

There is a parable in this for us. When we were created, something good was planted deep within us. That something good is the image or likeness of God. But for the God image or God likeness to grow within us, we have to give it room to grow. And we have to nurture it by being in fellowship with God through prayer and worship, listening for God's word to speak to us, striving to be loving and caring like God has been to us.

FOLLOW-UP: Lead the children in filling clear plastic soft drink bottles with potting soil and seeds to make terrariums. Plan it so some plants will need to be freed from the terrariums and planted outdoors so they can continue to grow.

94

38
Who Likes a Picnic?
We Can Learn a Lesson from the Ants

SCRIPTURE: Acts 5:42 GNT

OBJECT FOR SHARING: A picnic basket or picnic blanket, perhaps containing some appropriate "picnic snacks" for later.

PRESENTATION: This lesson works well at the end of spring or during summer, when picnics are on the minds of all. It can also be used when the theme of the day is evangelism or outreach.

How many of you like picnics? Most of us do. You know what else likes picnics? Ants do. Have you ever seen ants on your picnic table or blanket? I have too.

Today I have a story for you about picnic ants. One time a group of people were having a church picnic. They had taken along tea to drink. Since some people like their tea really, really, sweet, they had also taken along a sugar bowl.

Before long the picnickers noticed a single ant working among some sugar that had been spilled on the table. After eating his fill, the ant left the spilled sugar carrying one tiny grain of sugar.

But that is not the end of the story. A few minutes later, the ant returned with a dozen or so more ants. What do you think caused them to do that? Right, the first ant went and told them about the sweet treat he or she had found. These ants also went to the spilled sugar, ate their fill, and then walked off the table to their hole in the ground.

But wait, there is more. Pretty soon the picnickers noticed a whole army of ants marching across the picnic table to the spilled sugar. What started with one ant's discovery led to a sweet time for an entire colony of ants.

You know, I think there is some wisdom in that story for us. We come here from our homes, just like the first ant came from his or her home, and we find things here that make us feel good. We learn new ideas, we have fun, we get to be with friends, and we often get to eat good food (like ants at a picnic, you know). And then we go back to our homes, our schools, our playgrounds, and probably most of us never think about telling others what a good time we have at church.

But just think of how great it would if we would follow the example of the little ant and go back to our schools, playgrounds, and other places and tell them about the sweet time we find here at our church. Pretty soon we might see a whole army of kids coming up for children's parable.

FOLLOW-UP: 1) Spread out a picnic blanket for the children to sit on in a circle (more than one will be required if the group is large). Distribute appropriate "picnic snacks" from the basket and encourage each child to recount a special picnic. 2) Encourage the children to think of ways they can engage in appropriate forms of evangelism (inviting friends at school to religious education classes, special church events, Christmas pageants).

39
A Thing of Remembrance
Special Objects Help Us Remember Those We Love

SCRIPTURE: Psalm 112:6 GNT

OBJECT FOR SHARING: Any object—a hand tool, picture frame, item of jewelry, vase, piece of china—that was given by a loved one who has died and that holds special meaning for the presenter.

PRESENTATION: The most appropriate Sunday for this story is Memorial Sunday, though it could be adapted for All Saints Sunday.

Good morning! Have you ever seen one of these? I thought this object might be of interest to you, and that is one of the reasons I brought it with me this morning. What do you suppose this object is used for?

Well, this is a combination hand drill/power screwdriver. You can insert a drill bit and then drill a small hole. When would this come in handy? That's correct. Suppose I am out in the backyard and need to drill a hole, but I don't have an electric drill. I can use this to drill a hole without electricity. But in the olden days, carpenters *always* had to drill and saw without electricity.

Now, after I have drilled my hole, I insert a screwdriver bit and use it as a power screwdriver. It makes it a lot quicker and easier.

But there is another reason that I brought this object with me this morning. This hand drill and screwdriver was given to me by my late grandfather, who was a carpenter, about twenty-five years ago. My grandfather died in 1989. So, you see, this object is very special to me. Because whenever I use this screwdriver/hand drill, I remember him. And remembering is good. The memories we have of our loved ones who are no longer with us is one of life's greatest blessings.

Today is Memorial Sunday. Tomorrow is Memorial Day. This weekend we are reminded to remember those loved ones who are no longer with us. That is what the word "memorial" means—something to help us remember some person or event. But we are especially encouraged to remember this weekend those who died for the cause of what is right, those who died for the sake of justice, and those who died to secure and preserve freedom.

So, this weekend I encourage each of you—adults included—to look around your home and focus on some of the objects you have that remind you of loved ones who have died. Then, maybe you will want to say a short prayer of thanks for the way those loved ones blessed your life.

FOLLOW-UP: 1) Encourage the children to remember and draw a picture of a special loved one. 2) Ask them to make a list of things in their home that were passed down from loved ones. To do so leads them to remember. 3) Lead the children in a closing prayer of thanks for loved ones who have died, but who blessed their lives.

40
Windsocks of the Spirit
The Spirit Is Revealed within Us

SCRIPTURE: John 6:63 GNT

OBJECT FOR SHARING: A colorful (red if possible) lawn wind-sock.

PRESENTATION: Plan this story for Pentecost Sunday (fifty days after Easter). Position a good household fan for effectiveness.

Good morning! Where do you think you might see one of these *(hold up windsock for all to see)*? In someone's lawn, at a weather station, or at an airport. All of those answers are correct.

Let's think about the windsocks that we might see at an airport, especially a small airport. Why, do you suppose, a windsock is needed at an airport? Well, it is because when a pilot is about to land a plane, she or he needs to know how strong the wind is and the direction it is coming from. A pilot can't just look out the window of the airplane and see the wind to determine these things, because, as we all know, the wind is invisible. But a windsock catches the wind and shows the pilot and those in the control tower if the wind is calm or strong and from which direction it is coming.

I thought we would try an experiment this morning. Let's see if this windsock actually works. I have brought some artificial wind *(turn on the fan and hold the windsock in front of the breeze)*. See how the wind fills the sock and shows the direction of the wind?

Now, why this lesson on wind and windsocks? Well, today is Pentecost Sunday. The scriptures tell us that on that first Pentecost Sunday long ago, God's Spirit swooped down upon the followers of Jesus like a mighty, rushing wind. And all the believers were filled with the Spirit, which enabled them to speak in other languages.

We believe that the Spirit is with us here today, too. We don't expect the rush of a mighty wind like that miracle long ago. Nevertheless, the Spirit is here. But we cannot see the Spirit, can we? We cannot reach out and grab the Spirit. So how does the Spirit reveal itself? Just as the wind is invisible and can only be seen when it fills something like the windsock, the Spirit is invisible and can only be seen when it fills something too. And you know what that thing is that the Spirit fills? It is you and I—people who love God. How does the Spirit reveal itself in us? By the loving, caring, forgiving, kindly things that we do for others. When we do these things that Jesus asks us to do, the Spirit shows itself to be in us.

So then, you might say that we are God's windsocks. Windsocks of the Spirit, that's what we are, when we let the Spirit blow through us.

FOLLOW-UP: The ambitious leader can purchase suitable fabric at a fabric store and help the children make a windsock for the church gardens as a continual reminder of the lesson.

Notes

1. Leonard Sweet.
2. Randy Hammer, *Everyone a Butterfly: 40 Sermons for Children*. (Boston: Skinner House Books, 2004), vi–ix.
3. Adapted from an ancient wisdom story, "At the City Gates," source unknown, from Margaret Silf, ed., *Wisdom Stories from Around the World*. (Cleveland: Pilgrim Press, 2003).
4. Retelling of a traditional story, "God in Hiding," source unknown, from Margaret Silf, ed., *Wisdom Stories from Around the World*. (Cleveland: Pilgrim Press, 2003).

Annotated Resources

Anderson, Herbert, and Foley, Edward. *Mighty Stories, Dangerous Rituals: Weaving Together the Human and the Divine*. San Francisco: Jossey-Bass, 1998.
    Discusses the power of religious ritual and myth and how they help us create and express meaning. Shows how ritual and myth connect the human and divine.

Bettelheim, Bruno. *The Uses of Enchantment: The Meaning and Importance of Fairy Tales*. New York: Alfred A. Knopf, 1976.
    An invaluable resource in the theory of how children's tales should arouse curiosity, stimulate the imagination, help children discover their self-identity and deal with inner conflicts, and confront their fears and problems.

Cameron, Julia. *The Artist's Way*. New York: G.P. Putnam's Sons, 1992.
    Cameron seeks, through practical guidance, to bring out the creative energy, what she refers to as "God energy," that is within all of us.

Campbell, Joseph. With Bill Moyers. *The Power of Myth*. New York: Doubleday, 1988.
    This work highlights exactly what the title suggests: the power of religious myths. Much is said about the hero that "lurks in each one of us."

Coles, Robert. *The Spiritual Life of Children*. Boston: Houghton Mifflin Company, 1990.
   A wealth of wisdom has been gleaned and shared from Coles' interviews with hundreds of children from a number of religious backgrounds. This work reveals the great depth of thought in religious matters that children are capable of when given a chance to express themselves.

Estes, Clarissa Pinkola, ed. *Tales of the Brothers Grimm*. New York: Quality Paperback Book Club, 1999.
   In her introduction to the *Tales of the Brothers Grimm*, Estes discusses soul life, innate ideals, and universal thoughts. A good resource for those interested in universal thoughts and archetypes.

Fahs, Sophia L. *Jesus the Carpenter's Son*. Boston: Beacon Press, 1945.
   Fahs uses the imagination (and indirectly encourages the modern presenter of children's sermons) to fill in the blanks and address the "What ifs" that surround the life of Jesus.

Fahs, Sophia. L. *Today's Children and Yesterday's Heritage*. Boston: Beacon, 1952.
   In this work Fahs stresses the importance of a child's self-worth, the child's sense of relationship with the larger world, the need to "feel the Mystery of Life," and the interdependence of all life.

Groome, Thomas H. *Christian Religious Education*. San Francisco: Harper Collins, 1980.
   Groome speaks of the importance of lived faith, becoming what we are called to become, and nurturing human freedom and creativity.

Hammer, Randy. *Everyone a Butterfly: 40 Sermons for Children*. Boston: Skinner House Books, 2004.
   In addition to forty children's sermons that follow the church year beginning in September and ending in June, this collection includes an introduction that discusses the theory of sermon preparation for children and what makes for a "successful" children's sermon. Following the same general format as the present volume, each entry includes a suggested object for sharing, suggestions for presentation, and possible follow-up activities.

Handford, S.A., translator. *Aesop's Fables*. New York: Penguin, 1994.
   Brief moral tales, many of which can easily be adapted for use with children in worship. In the introduction, Handford discusses the "common-sense and folk wisdom" at the heart of stories and fables.

Harris, Maria. *Fashion Me a People*. Louisville: Westminster John Knox Press, 1989.
   Harris notes the importance of spending time alone "in the company of the Divine."

Jordan, Jerry Marshall. *Filling Up the Brown Bag* (a children's sermon how-to book). New York: Pilgrim Press, 1987.

An invaluable resource, Jordan stresses the importance of letting children know they are loved and wanted, nurturing within them an awareness of God, instilling within them a sense of self-worth and a positive self-image, encouraging them to stretch themselves and reach their full potential, and sparking their imaginations by getting them to say "I see!"

Rogers, Fred. *Play Time*. Philadelphia: Running Press, 2001.

A good resource, most notably for preschoolers, for planning follow-up activities utilizing common household objects. Encourages children's use of imagination and creativity.

Rogers, Fred. *You Are Special*. Philadelphia: Running Press, 2002.

A tiny pocket book of timeless wisdom that reinforces the truth that everyone is special and that can easily be worked into many children's sermons.

Wagner, Betty Jane. *Dorothy Heathcote: Drama as a Learning Medium*. Revised ed. Portland, Me.: Calendar Islands Publishers, 1999.

Though written as a resource for leading children in drama, this is also a good resource—especially the first half—on how to physically lead children's sermons. Discusses the discovery of human experience, reaching a deeper insight, helping children catch a vision of the wider world, and the importance of tapping the energy of the human spirit and valuing human achievement.

Silf, Margaret, ed. *Wisdom Stories from Around the World*. Cleveland: Pilgrim Press, 2003.

Though written primarily from an adult viewpoint, many of these wonderful stories can be adapted for use with children.

Supply List

Chapter 1: The Talking Stick
- Any kind of decorated stick

Chapter 2: The Potato Peeler
- Bowl
- Paring knife
- Potato

Chapter 3: What Are You Looking For?
- Crossing guard sign

Chapter 4: Eric Faces the Giant
- Popular style of lunchbox

Chapter 5: The Hospitable Squirrel
- Variety of nuts

Chapter 6: Playing in Harmony
- An Appalachian dulcimer
- Or other such interesting instrument that easily can be taken out of tune

Chapter 7: Giving to God First
- Wallet or purse
- One-dollar bills (play money can be used)

Chapter 8: The Sharecropper
- Several ears of corn

Chapter 9: Things that Make Us Think
- 🖐 Minister's red stole

Chapter 10: Taking Off Our Mask
- 🖐 Papier-mâché art mask, with the two sides painted differently
- 🖐 Or an appropriate Halloween mask

Chapter 11: Giving Our Best
- 🖐 Golf club or putter
- 🖐 Plastic golf ball

Chapter 12: The Big Job of Little Leaves
- 🖐 Colorful variety of fresh, fall leaves

Chapter 13: Many Ways to Honor God
- 🖐 A shoe last (perhaps can be borrowed from a local shoe repair shop)
- 🖐 Small hammer
- 🖐 Shoe

Chapter 14: A Cup of Cold Water
- 🖐 Small cups
- 🖐 Clear pitcher of cool water

Chapter 15: Preparing the Manger
- 🖐 Nativity set

Chapter 16: The Courageous Shepherd Boy
- 🖐 Religious statue, icon, or picture of a shepherd

Chapter 17: I Spy
- 🖐 Any objects of significance in the room or worship space that might not be readily observed

Chapter 18: The Good Shepherd
- 🖐 Statue, figurine, or picture of a shepherd

Chapter 19: Peacemakers
✋ Police officer's badge

Chapter 20: So Many Days on the Calendar
✋ New calendar with nature scenes

Chapter 21: Following a Star
✋ Icon, statue, or picture of the Magi

Chapter 22: Elephant in the Room
✋ Picture of an elephant

Chapter 23: Sun and Moon
✋ Round rock that can resemble the moon
✋ Small flashlight
✋ Mirror

Chapter 24: Who Can Be a Poet?
✋ Picture of poet Phyllis Wheatley

Chapter 25: God's Special Hiding Place
✋ Heart-shaped candy box

Chapter 26: Not Like You
✋ Variety of seeds—sunflower seed, pumpkin seed, watermelon seed, peach pit, apple seed, pear seed, acorn, maple seed, etc
✋ Bowl

Chapter 27: Invite FRANC to Church
✋ Small index cards, with these words written on them:

Invite to church:
F riends
R elatives
A cquaintances
N eighbors
C lub members

Chapter 28: A Special Kind of Book

- Sample of Braille text

Chapter 29: A Rock in My Shoe

- Small pebble

Chapter 30: A Special Place

- Objects—religious or personal—that help bring calm to the soul

Chapter 31: A Special Parade

- Palm branches
- Robe, coat, or cloak

Chapter 32: Full or Empty?

- Basket
- Plastic Easter eggs filled with candy
- One empty plastic Easter egg

Chapter 33: Eric's Baseball Glove

- Old, tattered baseball glove
- New baseball glove

Chapter 34: Keeping a Proper Focus

- Small picture of Jesus
- Magnifying glass

Chapter 35: Seeds of God

- A children's Bible
- Any variety of seeds

Chapter 36: A Special Tree

- Plaque that honors someone

Chapter 37: Letting God Grow

- Acorn or other seed that has sprouted in a terrarium jar

Chapter 38: Who Likes a Picnic?

- Picnic basket or blanket
- Picnic snacks

Chapter 39: A Thing of Remembrance

- A hand tool or other object that holds special meaning because it was given by a loved one who has died

Chapter 40: Windsocks of the Spirit

- Red or other colorful lawn windsock

About the Author

Randy Hammer

Randy Hammer has over thirty years of experience in pastoral ministry. He has worked with children in Vacation Church School, outdoor ministry, and of course, during the children's sermon time. His number one passion in ministry has been the preparation and delivery of sermons. Other passions include writing poetry and devotional materials, woodworking, and spending time with his wife, children, and their grandchildren.

He is the author of *Dancing in the Dark: Lessons in Facing Life's Challenges with Courage and Creativity* (1999, The Pilgrim Press) and *Everyone a Butterfly: Forty Sermons for Children*, (2004, Skinner House).

OTHER BOOKS FROM THE PILGRIM PRESS

SHOW ME A PICTURE: *30 Children's Sermons Using Visual Arts*
Phyllis Vos Wezeman and Anna L. Liechty
ISBN 0-8298-1636-4/paper/96 pages/$12.00

TELL ME A STORY: *30 Children's Sermons Based on Best-Loved Books*
Phyllis Vos Wezeman and Anna L. Liechty
ISBN 0-8298-1635-6/paper/96 pages/$12.00

WIPE THE TEARS: *30 Children's Sermons on Death*
Phyllis Vos Wezeman, Anna L. Liechty, and Kenneth R. Wezeman
ISBN 0-8298-1520-1/paper/96 pages/$10.00

TASTE THE BREAD: *30 Children's Sermons on Communion*
Phyllis Vos Wezeman, Anna L. Liechty, and Kenneth R. Wezeman
ISBN 0-8298-1519-8/paper/96 pages/$10.00

TOUCH THE WATER: *30 Children's Sermons on Baptism*
Phyllis Vos Wezeman, Anna L. Liechty, and Kenneth R. Wezeman
ISBN 0-8298-1518-X/112 pages/paper/$10.00

PLANTING SEEDS OF FAITH
Virginia H. Loewen
ISBN 0-8298-1473-6/96 pages/paper/$10.00

GROWING SEEDS OF FAITH
Virginia H. Loewen
ISBN 0-8298-1488-4/96 pages/paper/$10.00

THE BROWN BAG
Jerry Marshall Jordan
ISBN 0-8298-0411-0/117 pages/paper/$9.95

SMALL WONDERS: *Sermons for Children*
Glen E. Rainsley
ISBN 0-8298-1252-0/104 pages/paper/$12.95

TIME WITH OUR CHILDREN: *Stories for Use in Worship, Year B*
Dianne E. Deming
ISBN 0-8298-0952-X/182 pages/paper/$9.95

TIME WITH OUR CHILDREN: *Stories for Use in Worship, Year C*
Dianne E. Deming
ISBN 0-8298-0953-8/157 pages/paper/$9.95

To order these or any other books from The Pilgrim Press call or write to:
The Pilgrim Press
700 Prospect Avenue East, Cleveland, Ohio 44115-1100
Phone orders: 1-800-537-3394 • Fax orders: 216-736-2206

Please include shipping charges of $4.00 for the first book and $0.75 for each additional book.
Or order from our web sites at www.pilgrimpress.com and www.ucpress.com.
Prices subject to change without notice.